TECHNOLOGY and UNION SURVIVAL

DISCARDED

TECHNOLOGY and UNION SURVIVAL
A Study of the Printing Industry

DANIEL T. SCOTT

PRAEGER

New York
Westport, Connecticut
London

Library of Congress Cataloging-in-Publication Data

Scott, Daniel T.
    Technology and union survival.

    Bibliography: p.
    Includes index.
    1. Printing industry--Technological innovations.
2. Trade-unions--Printing industry   I. Title.
Z243.A2S35 1987   331.88'116862   87-2334
ISBN 0-275-92680-X (alk. paper)

Copyright © 1987 by Praeger Publishers

All rights reserved. No portion of this book may be
reproduced, by any process or technique, without the
express written consent of the publisher.

Library of Congress Catalog Card Number: 87-2334
ISBN: 0-275-92680-X

First published in 1987

Praeger Publishers,
521 Fifth Avenue, New York, NY 10175
A division of Greenwood Press, Inc.

Printed in the United States of America

∞

The paper used in this book complies with the
Permanent Paper Standard issued by the National
Information Standards Organization (Z39.48-1984).

10 9 8 7 6 5 4 3 2 1

To Joan, Walter, and Darby

SHATFORD LIBRARY

NOV   2000

PASADENA CITY COLLEGE
1570 E. COLORADO BLVD
PASADENA, CA 91106

Acknowledgements

One of the most satisfying tasks of an author is to acknowledge the help of people who made the work possible. While space does not allow mentioning all who have assisted in this endeavor, certain individuals have provided substantial help with this book.

Expert information and industry data has been freely provided by Charlie Alessandrini, Dick Anderson, Robert Baker, Mike Bruno, Charles Cook, Robert Critchlow, Donald Daniels, William Friday, Brian Gill, J. Llamas, Daniel Loftus, William Lofquist, William Lamparte, Donald Piercy, Donald Ramstad, Ford Ray, Frank J. Romano, Robert L. Schweiger, John W. Seybold, George Silvestri, Bill Solomon, Elman Snow, Tom Shirk and John Trieste.

Valuable insights and suggestions have been tirelessly given by Mike Coulson, Nelson Eldred, Jim Horne, Dennis Molloy and Jack Simich. Ching and Tom Lacey, as well as Gerry Scott, have provided numerous useful comments over the life of this study. Professors Ross Thomson and David Gordon have offered valuable advice and searching criticism. In particular, my dissertation committee chairman, Professor David Schwartzman, has provided continued support and direction from this project's inception. Jean Najdzin and Carol Stock have carefully prepared the manuscript for publication.

To all of them I express my thanks.

Contents

List of Tables

List of Diagrams

Introduction

This analysis of the decline in the unionization of the commercial printing industry, through comparison and evaluation of historical trends in craft union membership, provides a new analytical framework supported by data on craft training requirements and employment not previously available.

This work deals with the way in which advances in production technology introduce new forms of competition into the craft union labor market. In so doing, two case studies are presented showing how the International Typographical Union (ITU) and Graphic Communications International Union (GCIU) responded to that competition. This study's evaluation of these responses ascribes the decline in printing union membership to the new technology and the resistance of both the ITU and GCIU to the substitution of lower skilled labor in traditional craft functions.

Why has printing union membership continually declined since 1969? Union membership grew in the previous 25 years despite the introduction of linotype, automatic feeding, and lithographic processes. What most distinguishes the period presently under study from the previous period is the often dramatic reduction of skill required by the new printing production processes, resulting from an evolution from craft work to the self-controlled production process of photocomposition, photo-direct offset, and electrophotography.

In tracing the effects of skill reduction, this study examines the disproportionate decrease in union membership during a period of increasing printing industry employment. The combined memberships of the commercial branches of the ITU and GCIU declined from 154,700 to 99,200 in the 14-year period between 1969 and 1983. During the same period, commercial printing (SIC 275) production employment increased from 272,600 to 318,900, while industry unionization declined from 58 percent in 1969 to 31 percent in 1983.

This study draws together in a single analytical framework the interactions of production technology, occupational skill, and union policies and the effects on craft union membership. Chapter 1 presents the craft union response model as the framework for analyzing the decline in unionization. This model shows how labor union policies mediate the

influence of exogenous technology upon union membership. By determining the level of operator skill, new technology determines the
demand for process skills. Technological change, the first determinant,
alters the proportional employment of skilled and unskilled labor and,
together with the union response to variations in the demand for craft
labor, it determines the proportion of industry unionization. The craft
model provides for a second determinant of union employment and
wages: trade union policy. Through this variable, union policies can
expand the number of jobs under contract by adopting an industrial
union structure and organizing competitive labor. In other terms, the
consequence of new technology on union employment is modified or
reversed depending upon the success of union policies in expanding the
number of positions included in union contracts. Chapter 4 considers a
third determinant of union membership, management resistance,
through a review of the literature.

The craft union response model implies three working hypotheses.
The first two hypotheses explain the influence of technological change,
and the third, influence of craft union policy. This study hypothesizes
that a series of minor technological innovations have reduced the level
of skill required in traditional printing craft production. Second, it is
hypothesized that, in addition to minor technological innovations, three
major new processes have reduced the proportional craftworker employment in particular operations and might change the distribution
between operations as some products expand relative to others. The
third hypothesis states that printing unions have increased relative
union/nonunion wage rates in response to both partial and complete
skill displacement, respectively.

The first and second hypotheses are that, in the production of
printed matter, technological change reduces or eliminates the level of
craftworker skill required for printed matter. Chapter 2 tests the first
set of hypotheses by separately comparing the necessary skills of the
typesetting, preparation and press workers between 1958 and the date
of each new process introduction. The partial skill displacing properties
of cathode ray tube (CRT) photocomposition on each function of the
typesetter's craft is then evaluated. This chapter also details the complete skill displacing properties of photo-direct offset and electrostatic
processes, as well as the partial skill displacement of the four minor
innovations upon preparation and press crafts.

Chapter 3 quantifies the historical transformation from craft to
unskilled printing production. Support for the skill-decline hypothesis
is sought in the decline in craftworker training requirements that
accompanied the introduction of the innovations concerned. The years
of training in both union and nonunion apprenticeships between 1948
and 1982 is related to the introduction of specific technology. Then a

composite measure of printing craft skill decline is developed by weighting the number of years of training with the comparable percent of industry craft occupational employment.

In order to test for complete skill displacement, however, a different method is necessary to quantify the increase in the substitution of unskilled for craft production labor. The printers' skill index does not consider new processes that require only unskilled operations. Moreover, the decline in proportional craft employment is measured by estimating the relative employment growth of private and quick printers utilizing new, unskilled processes.

To further test the union membership model, two case studies are presented of the ITU and GCIU, the two remaining national printing unions. The ITU traditionally represents typesetting or composing room workers. The GCIU is an umbrella organization representing printing workers employed in the preparation, press, and bindery functions. Chapters 4 and 5 detail union policy responses to technological change, as well as their influence upon the unionization of the typesetting and printing sectors of the labor market.

This craft union membership model allows for the interaction and separate analysis of the three historical union responses to technological change. Paradoxically, while the restructuring of unions and the organization of competitive labor potentially expand the number of union positions, uneconomic work rules tend to block the substitution of unskilled labor in traditional craft functions. Consequently, these work rules reduce union employment opportunities. The journeyman work rule requires that craftsmen who operate any new equipment that is able to perform the functions of journeymen be paid at rates of pay and terms of employment equal to those of journeymen themselves.

Chapter 4 tests the third hypothesis, which states that the ITU and GCIU maintain relative skilled union membership wages in response to displacement of craft skills. This analysis first compares the historical variation in the relative wages of the skilled membership of the ITU and GCIU with the earnings of all manufacturing workers. The chapter also tests this last hypothesis by comparing the relative union/nonunion new process operator wage rates in the typesetting and printing labor market sectors of the ITU and GCIU, respectively.

Finally, Chapter 5 draws together the analysis of technological change and union policies into the two historical case studies of the ITU and GCIU. The chronological relation of new process introduction, craftworker training, proportional skilled employment, and union membership is considered from the two perspectives of the typesetting sector of the ITU and the printing labor market sector of the GCIU. The chapter concludes by suggesting some implications of a continually evolving technology for future industry unionization.

1

Union Membership Decline Model

INTRODUCTION

This chapter provides an overview of the major structural mechanisms that influence the historical variation in craft union memberships. The *craft union membership model* is introduced, which hypothesizes that union membership varies directly with both changes in skill requirements of production technology, and with craft union responses to the resultant variations in demand for skilled employment.

This model offers an explanation for the historical decline in membership of printing craft unions. A unified theory shall be presented to explain the structural decline in printing union craft membership since 1969, in order to isolate causation in the long-term structural relations between technology and skilled union membership and thus increase the possibility of projecting trends in union membership.

The craft union membership model presented here attempts a synthesis of certain elements, until now only fragmented in the literature, concerning the influence of technology and union policy upon craft union membership.

The construction of this model begins with a description of the two mechanisms that reflect variations in both technology and union policy. By altering demand for process skills, technological change varies the proportional demand between skilled and unskilled labor. Relative union/nonunion wages are the mechanisms through which union printers respond to technological change. The model implies that by maintaining relative union/nonunion wage rates, union printers contribute to their own membership decline.

1

Within the context of the craft union response model, three hypotheses explain the relationship between technology, occupational skill, craft employment, union policy, and printing union membership.

Structure of Craft Union Membership Decline

This study hypothesizes that the historical decline in printing craft union membership is caused by new process introduction, as well as by the response of craft unions to technological change. New process introduction begins the transformation of the once predominantly unionized craft labor market; union policies contribute to that continuing transformation. Therefore, it is technology that transforms the occupational structure of the printing industry from a reliance on craft labor to a need for unskilled employment. By responding to the introduction of processes requiring less skill with work rules that block unskilled membership and result in ineffective membership recruitment, union policies contribute to the decline in the unionization of the printing labor market.

The structure of union membership decline is depicted in terms of a simple process diagram. As indicated in Diagram 1.1, technology begins the transformation (left) which is completed with the degree of labor market unionization (right). Technology alters the demand for occupational skills, while the influence of new processes is mediated by three union policies. New printing processes determine the demand for both craft and unskilled employment as well as the level of craft skill required. The introduction of new technology reduces the number of craft skills and permits the substitution of unskilled labor. This results in a decline in the required level and proportion of craft employment.

Two general types of technological change directly reduce the demand for production skills required in the printing industry. The first is the introduction of automatic process control. Electrophotography, photo-direct offset (sometimes termed the copy-to-plate method), and digital cathode ray tube (CRT) composition are the three major self-controlled innovations altering the demand for printing skills. For example, CRT photocomposition allows the previously skilled functions of word hyphenation, line justification, and page make-up to be controlled by digital computers. In the pressroom, computerized press consoles "read" and automatically correct errors.[1]

The second type of technological change is the mechanization of hand operations. In this instance, camera, platemaking, and press hand skills, which once required long training periods to develop, have now been displaced by automated equipment.[2]

DIAGRAM – 1.1. CRAFT UNION MEMBERSHIP MODEL

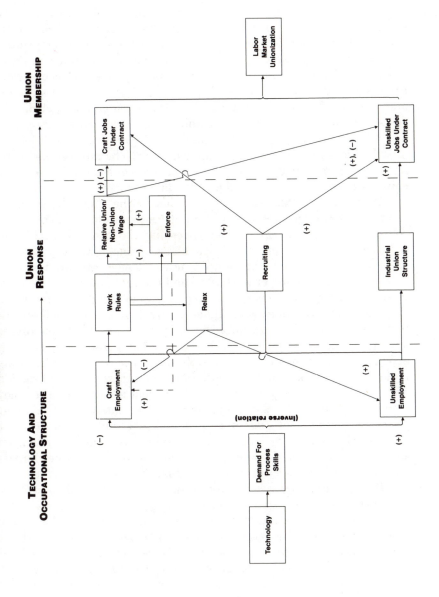

Because of these two types of technological change, membership is determined by the responses of printing unions both to the redefinition of craft as it reflects less need for skill and to the consequent increase in need for relatively unskilled labor. The self-controlled process of CRT photocomposition and the mechanization of hand operations in the nontypesetting sector reduced the level of skill required, and by so doing changed the definition of printing crafts. Similarly, the two self-controlled processes of electrophotography and photo-direct offset entirely displaced craft production methods for single-color printing, and consequently increased the proportional demand for unskilled operators. Historically, union printers have responded to technological change with work rules, conversion from craft to industrial structure, and new membership recruitment. The three trade union policies discussed herein affect labor market unionization through the intermediate determination of the total number of both craft positions and unskilled jobs included within union contracts. The intervening analytical step permits union policies to expand or contract union membership as a proportion of the total printing labor market.

Work rules within union plants embody the choice between two competing union goals: maximization of wages or employment. In the collective bargaining agreements governing the commercial printing industry, work rules are the mechanisms through which wages and employment are varied. Diagram 1.1 indicates how this variation operates. Given a relaxation of work rules and the consequent decline in the relative union/nonunion wage, union policy would tend to increase both the skilled and unskilled jobs under contract. If a union enforces the payment of a skilled wage for either a lower or unskilled new process operation, then the union has chosen customary rates of pay at the expense of employment. The returning influence of work rules is also indicated in the diagrammed relation between these rules and the jobs under contract. Initially, work rule enforcement increases craft employment but, because of the consequential higher relative union/nonunion wages, the number of craft and unskilled jobs under union contract declines. Over a period of time, the relatively higher union wage encourages the substitution of nonunion craft labor and unskilled new process operators in traditional union craft positions.

Instead of enforcement, union printers might respond to new, less skill-intensive technology by relaxing the requirement that only skilled craftsmen perform work in traditional craft functions. The cost of relaxing work rules by permitting the employment of the unskilled in new process operations would be an initial reduction in the number of craft workers. The relaxation of work rules within union plants would displace craft workers employed at customary rates of pay with less skilled labor employed at significantly lower pay.

Union policies can expand the number of jobs under contract by both adopting an industrial structure and recruiting new membership. Industrial restructuring is the expansion of single craft unions to include a larger number of crafts within that union's jurisdiction, as well as the addition of unskilled workers to its membership which would allow the printing unions to contractually control more job opportunities. While the expansion in the eligibility of membership and the recruitment of competitive labor potentially expand the number of union positions, uneconomic work rules increase the relative union/nonunion wage. This, in turn, decreases union employment opportunities by requiring a more highly skilled craft worker where an unskilled operator is sufficient.

By encompassing all three possible union policies, the process diagram demonstrates the potential for a combination of initiatives in the face of new process introduction. For example, work rules might initially limit the operation of new process equipment to displaced craftsmen until the skill requirement of the new process is established. Expanding the jurisdiction of the union to include the unskilled would keep control of the process within union jurisdiction. The organization of competitive labor would tend to protect any relative union wage advantage.

Craft Union Membership Model

Printing union membership in the craft union membership model is determined by two variables: (1) the technological demand for process skills; and (2) the union response to new process introduction. All other things being equal, the proportion of craft employment is determined by the demand for process skills. Given the proportional distribution between craft and unskilled employment, union policies influence the number of jobs under contract and, as a consequence of this, the degree of unionization in the printing labor market. This section shall illustrate, in a form suggested by Eagly, how the proportion of craft employment is determined by production technology, and how union policies determine union membership.[3]

While technology and union policy are the ultimate determinants, the direct determinants of unionization are the employment of craftsmen and the relative union/nonunion wage. Over the long run, as a percentage of the total labor market, craft union membership (U) is determined by the proportional employment of craftsmen (E) and the relative union/nonunion hourly wage rate (W). Therefore, it can be said that:

$$U = f(E, W) \tag{1}$$

The employment of craftsmen, moreover, is determined by the technological demand for production skills. The measure of occupational skills demanded in performing a given operation (S) is dependent upon technology (T), which is exogenously determined:

$$S = s(T) \quad \text{where} \quad \frac{\partial S}{\partial T} \leq 0 \tag{2}$$

The demand for craft occupational skills decreases with the skill requirement of new production technology. If technological change displaced one set of comparable skills for another, that is,

$$\frac{\partial S}{\partial T} = 0, \tag{3}$$

then the demand for craft occupational skill would not diminish. The changing proportion of craftsmen employed (E) in the labor market is dependent upon the change in skill (S). Therefore,

$$E = e(S) \quad \text{where} \quad \frac{\partial E}{\partial S} \geq 0 \tag{4}$$

Employment of craftsmen will remain constant if one set of craft skills is substituted for another or if employment declines in conjunction with a decrease in the demand for craft occupational skills. Since the craft union membership model only considers the possibility of stable or declining skill requirements, the case of increasing skill requirements does not imply an increase in the employment of skilled printers.

Union response to skill reductions that accompany technological change is a qualitative variable that can only be indirectly measured. Work rule enforcement, the primary union response to technological change, may be represented as:

$$W = w(P) \tag{5}$$

Relative union wages are a function of International Typographical Union (ITU) and Graphic Communications International Union (GCIU) policy. The variable (p) is the union preference for wages rather than employment. The relative union/nonunion hourly wage rate (w) is a measure of the union policy response to a variation in occupational skill.

Union policy determines total membership through its influence upon both the number of craft positions and the number of unskilled jobs under contract. Empirically, this study will show further on how the substitution of craftworkers with less skilled labor occurs. Unionization of the labor market will decline if the relative union wage increases. Conversely, it will not decline if the relative union/nonunion wage rate remains constant. While the craft union model only considers the possibilities of constant or increasing relative wages, it should be noted that the case of a declining relative union wage does not necessarily imply an increase in the number of craft positions and unskilled jobs under contract.

The derived relation between union membership (U), the demand for process skills (T) as well as union policy (P) is:

$$U = u(e[sT]), w(P) \qquad \qquad (6)$$

In determining the number of occupational skills, technology determines the proportion of skilled and unskilled labor and, in turn, causes a variation in the number of skilled union members. Union policy, the second qualitative variable, influences total union membership indirectly through its influence on the relative union/nonunion wage rate. Given the initially high proportion of craft membership, the historical trend in printing labor market unionization is dependent upon the variation in both the proportion of skilled workers and the relative union/nonunion wage rates.

The variable relationships implied in the craft union membership model can be tested in a series of three hypotheses. The relation between technology, occupational skill, and craft employment is tested in the first two hypotheses by describing and measuring the change in occupational skills before and after new process introduction. The second set of two hypotheses tests the relation of union policy as embodied in relative wages to the hypothesized partial and full occupational skill displacement. Each of the three hypotheses are then separately tested within the ITU typesetting and GCIU nontypesetting sectors of the labor market.

The first hypothesis is that technological change has reduced the level of skill required in craft production. Specifically, technology has either partially displaced or entirely displaced the craft skills of typesetting, preparation, and press operation. The link between technology and skill is first tested by comparing the skills in the typesetting and nontypesetting sectors before and after new process introduction. Since technology reduces some and entirely displaces other craft skills, two separate measures of printing production skill are used. The printers' skill index measures craft redefinition caused by partial skill displacement. The variation in the proportion of unskilled production labor measures the complete displacement of craft skills.

The printers' craft skill index tests the craft decline hypothesis which states that technological change has partially displaced, or reduced, the craft skills of typesetting, preparation, and press craft workers. The effect of only one self-controlled new process (CRT photocomposition) and the mechanization of hand operations is measured in the reduction in the number of years of training required in craft apprenticeship. The printers' skill index measures the combined influence of reduction in particular craft training and the relative occupational employment of printing craft workers.

The relative earnings of skilled nonunion printers also tests the hypothesized decline in printing production craft skills. It is expected that the craft nonunion average hourly earnings in the commercial printing industry relative to all manufacturing workers will decline, together with printing craft skill index values.

The second hypothesis considers those cases in which technological change completely displaces printing craft skills. It is hypothesized that simplified new processes have reduced the proportional craftworker employment in particular operations, and might change the distribution between operations as some products expand relative to others. It is expected that the overall proportion of craft labor will decline but not necessarily in any particular labor market sector.

The third hypothesis is that the ITU and GCIU policies of maintaining relative skilled membership wages in response to partial and complete displacement has led to a decline in union membership. The effect of union work rules that require higher relative union/nonunion wage rates for new process operation is tested in both the case of partial and complete craft skill displacement. In the case of occupational skill decline, if the union skilled wage rate is constant relative to those of nonunion workers in general, then it is expected that union employment will decline. In order to test the union response to partial skill displacement, the historical variation in relative wages of the skilled membership of the ITU and GCIU are compared with hourly earnings of all manufacturing workers. Variation in the relative union/nonunion new process operators' wage rates indicates union response to complete displacement of unskilled new process operation.

LITERATURE REVIEW

Economic literature suggests the craft union membership hypothesis. The body of economic literature concerning skill displacement of union membership is generally fragmented into the detailed consideration of either the relation of production technology and occupational skill, or the relation of skill and craft union membership. Only one author, George Barnett, in *Chapters on Machinery and Labor* describes the effect of new technology on three crafts and the union membership of these skilled trades through historical case study. This section first considers the relations between technology, occupational skill, and craft union membership. Subsequently, the influence upon membership of union responses to technological change is considered.

Relation of Technology and Craft Skill

Production technology is the single most important determinant of occupational skills according to Reynolds.[4] In the printing industry, skills are generally divided between the functions of composition, preparation and press. The ability to perform the tasks within each function is the principal requirement for the employment of compositors, preparation, and press workers.

The effect upon skill requirements of new production techniques varies enormously among innovations. Case studies have been conducted to determine the effects of new methods and equipment on skill requirements in industries such as oil and gas refining, electronic equipment, pulp and paper, slaughtering and meat packing, rubber tires and tubes, machine shop trades, and medical services. None of the results of these case studies show any indication of a sharp or consistent increase in skill requirements as a consequence of switching to newer techniques.[5]

Within the context of both newspaper and commercial printing industries, the literature has detailed the influence of new technology on the basis of surveys, trade literature and expert trade opinion. Authors Gennard and Dunn, Griffin, Kelber and Schlessinger, Smith, Rodgers and Friedman, cited below, argue that the introduction of photocomposition caused a decline in both typesetting craft requirements and skilled ITU membership. Baker, Munson, and Zimbalist recognized the consequences of skill reducing preparation and press innovations upon nontypesetting union craftsmen.

Prior to the introduction of third generation photocomposition, Kelber and Schlessinger identified both the job and skill displacing properties of new typesetting methods during the period 1945–63. This study, *Union Printers and Controlled Automation*, analyzed the response of the largest ITU local, New York Local No. 6. While the job displacing potential of photocomposition was large, the authors noted that New York Local No. 6 did not experience a loss of employment prior to 1963. Kelber and Schlessinger, however, concluded that the second generation phototypesetting equipment downgraded the craft linotype operators' skills.[6]

In 1980, Rodgers and Friedman evaluated the rapid decline in ITU membership in the years between 1969 and 1976. They predicted that electronic photocomposition would end the life of New York Local No. 6 as a single craft union. After sampling both working and retired printers in 1976, these two sociologists concluded that electronic photo-composition had caused a decline in craft skills, union job opportunities, and membership.[7]

Zimbalist chronicles the further deskilling of the compositor's craft after the introduction of third generation photo-composition equipment. While Kelber and Schlessinger identify the reduction in typesetting skills, Zimbalist reviews how electronic data manipulation allows the creation of fully composed pages and obsolesces the make-up skills of the craft worker. Smith furthers this analysis by projecting the influence of newspaper photocomposition upon craftsmen and their union in the 1980s. Extrapolating the experience of the 1970s with electronic composition, Smith predicts that the skills of the typesetter will continue to decline drastically to lower levels.[8]

In an earlier study, Baker identifies the major trends in press work, prior to the actual decline in GCIU membership, that were ultimately to reduce the pressman's skill requirements. Writing in 1957, she describes the new pressroom technology as:

> ... new inks, electronic devices and precision instruments are constantly advancing these methods, reducing the need for continuous inspection and lowering production costs. More or less with success, the uncanny photoelectric eye starts and stops some press vibration, adjusts register, adjusts illuminating intensity and exercises other controls.[9]

While most literature focuses on the skill reducing properties of photocomposition, Zimbalist identifies the effect of new process controls on the pressman's crafts. Quoting the president of the pressmen's union, Zimbalist illustrates how new technology is making the printing press easier to operate. In addition to "obliterating the traditional craft skills of the printing trades" advancing technology, in the form of xerography, threatens to replace the printing press altogether.[10]

In a recent journal article, Gennard and Dunn trace the decline in craft control in the British printing industry between 1948 and 1982. These authors conclude that craft apprenticeship is no longer required in commercial printing and is evidenced by the growth of in-plant and instant printshops. "Outside of newspaper production," they state, "the new printing techniques require only a short period of training in composition, paste-up, and small litho printing to produce typesetting and printing at standards acceptable to customers."[11]

Relation of Occupational Skill Demand and Skilled Employment

The influence of technology upon skill displacement for the industry is first and most extensively analyzed in George Barnett's *Chapters on Machinery and Labor*. Barnett argues that within a competitive market, technological change determines the amount of skill displacement. The only market imperfection subsequently considered is the action of the affected trade unions and handworkers. Displacement from the trade is determined largely by "mechanical" and "economic" factors that center around the introduction of particular machines. Consequently, Barnett concludes that trade union policy affects skill displacement only within very narrow limits.[12]

While machinery affects the level of wages and unemployment, Barnett was rather concerned with a third effect of machinery—the displacement of skill, defined as the loss of the opportunity to pay acquired skill at the rate of remuneration that would have been received if the machine had not been introduced. "Displacement may take the form of employment loss or a lower rate of remuneration consequent to new machinery introduction."[13]

Barnett studies the effects of the introduction of four machines: the linotype, the stone planer, the semiautomatic bottle machine, and the automatic bottle machine. On the basis of the economic literature and four case studies, Barnett develops five factors that determine the extent of displacement upon skilled handworkers consequent to new process introduction. They are:

> (1) the rapidity of machine introduction; (2) mobility of labor within the skilled trade affected; (3) the effect of the machine in reducing the price of the manufactured article and thus increasing demand; (4) the labor displacing power of the machine; (5) the extent to which the skill of the handworker is useful in the machine process.[14]

The five factors that determine skill displacement are classified as either technological or economic. Technological factors displace skill at a rate determined by the rapidity of introduction and the labor-displacing power of the process. Economic factors salvage skill at a rate determined by the mobility of labor, increase in demand, and the degree to which handworker skill is useful consequent to the introduction of the new process.[15]

Useful as a starting point, the ambiguities of Barnett's analysis severely limit its application to technological change in the printing industry. The greatest flaw of Barnett's analysis is his imprecision with the element of time. Alfred Marshall noted that the nature of causality itself depends upon time. Since the purpose is to determine the structural relation between technology, skill, and union membership in the skilled printing trades, adequate time must be allowed for new processes to "work out undisturbed their full effect."[16] Specifically, enough time has to be allowed for changes to occur in the supply of skilled labor subsequent to the introduction of new production processes. Barnett did not develop the five determinants until 23 years after the introduction of the linotype was completed. Nevertheless, he does not distinguish between the long-term labor displacing power of the new process which is transforming the industry occupational structure and the four relatively short-term factors that only modify the labor displacement of new production technology.[17]

Barnett considered both the introduction of the linotype and the Owens automatic bottlemaker. Yet, *Chapters of Machinery and Labor* never distinguishes between the automation of hand skills and the use of self-controlled mechanisms that are essential to understanding the potential displacing power of new processes. Self-controlled equipment incorporates the process adjustment or decision-making responsibility that was formerly resident in the operator. The linotype automated the hand skills of the compositor, but it required a comparable level of skill to operate it. The Owens bottlemaker employed self-controlling mechanisms and reduced the level of operation to that of unskilled labor.[18]

Other than the labor displacing power of the machine, Barnett's four additional factors are of secondary importance in the relative short-run of particular industry studies. Identifying the rate of new machinery introduction is more useful if the process of innovation is discrete rather than a continuous evolution such as the digitation of all printing images which began with the application of binary electronic data processing to printing production. Barnett only considered self-contained innovations such as the linotype. As the effects of particular new processes become more pervasive, the rate of new process introduction becomes more continuous, and thus more difficult to identify and measure.

According to Barnett, the mobility of skilled labor and the usefulness of displaced handworker skills are two additional factors determining the number of displaced craftsmen.[19] Yet, the effectiveness of both these ameliorating factors depends upon the introduction of new production processes within distinct labor markets. Barnett allows for new substitute processes but does not consider the emergence of substitute suppliers. To the extent that new processes are employed outside of the traditional trade by quick and private printers, the usefulness of intra-trade mobility and of the retraining of skilled workers is diminished.

Considering the influence of new production processes exclusively within the trade ignores the fact that plant and industry labor markets are linked in the product market. Labor markets are a system of interrelated markets. Events in any one of these markets ultimately condition and are conditioned by events in all other markets. Industry labor markets are joined by the possible alternative uses for the same labor and by the substitutability of different labor in producing the same output. Labor and product markets are linked by the transformation of labor into products.[20]

Barnett assumes that there is no change in consumer taste after the introduction of new production technology. All variation in demand is dependent on the ability of technology to lower the cost of production. Yet, Barnett never estimates unit cost in his four case studies but, rather, merely implies a lower labor cost on the basis of higher labor productivity. However, Barnett does conclude that the implied unit cost reduction was not a significant factor in offsetting the labor displacing influence of new technology.[21]

Relation of Craft Demand and Skilled Union Membership

The source of printing craft union power is its control over the supply of skills. Historically, union membership was dependent upon the requirement of craft skills in the printing production process. In discussing the Amalgamated Lithographers of America (ALA), Munson argues that as long as the ALA controlled the supply of printing skills, they could cope with the mobility of the product, the mobility of the operation, and the ease of entry into the industry. [22]

The labor supply available to an industry depends primarily on the length of training needed for that occupation.[23] In 1958, nonunion craft training was 6½ years for a compositor and 6 years for a preparation journeyman. The length of apprenticeship effectively made the occupational labor supply curve inelastic in the short run.

The role of the printing union in the labor market is undergoing a dramatic change from what it was in an earlier technological stage where craft skill was essential to the existence of the printing industry. The union is an integral, inseparable part of this industrial process. The union is not only a wage regulator, but is also an agent that converts unskilled, raw labor into a specific type of skill required by the printing industry. The institutional power of the union historically has been based upon the industry's need for craft labor. The institutional structure of the labor market permitted the unions to define jurisdiction, certify training, and serve as the industry's employment agency. In defining the relation between jobs and workers, unions controlled the labor supply.

Skill reduction altered the institutional relations between labor, management, and the industry as a whole. It enabled the employer to define jobs, train workers, and satisfy his or her own employment requirements. The core issue is whether labor or management controls the labor supply. Technological change permitted the employer to obtain adequate labor without recourse to the union's training and hiring structure. Technological change, therefore, ended the union's employment service. The literature suggests this latter relationship: that there is a rough, proportional relation between union power, union membership, and unionization of the industry's labor supply.[24]

Union membership rests on the ability of the union to stop production. The more skilled and specialized union members are, the more difficult it is for management to carry on production by using strike breakers or nonstriking management employees.[25] As technology erodes the demand for union craft skills, it simultaneously decreases union bargaining power.

Charles Craypo concluded that changing industrial technology undermines union bargaining power. As if describing the historical case of the printing industry after 1958, Craypo states that technology destroys ". . . the skill-based bargaining leverage of the traditional relevant work force as employers find they can substitute machinery for unskilled labor."[26]

UNION RESPONSES TO SKILL DISPLACEMENT

A review of the economic literature also identifies determinants—work rules and policies—governing the employment of craft union membership subsequent to technological change. It is seen that, given constant product demand, the long-term availability of union job opportunities is dependent upon work rules and policies that gain control over these industry employment opportunities.

Given the exogenous influence of technology upon the demand for process skills, there is a division in the location of union response: either traditional union jurisdictional boundaries are enlarged; or the union seeks to organize and control the larger competitive environment. Assuming traditional union jurisdictional boundaries, Barnett considers the effect of union work rules on the displacement of skilled hand craftsmen. Without the assumption of any collective bargaining or industry boundaries, Chandler, Munson, and Gennard and Dunn consider two alternative policy responses: either increasing the number of job opportunities under union control through a restructuring of membership to include both skilled and unskilled workers; or the organization of new process workers who, because of technological change, now function as substitutes for traditional craft workers. The following two sections consider both of these models, which are so named on the basis of the primary union response mechanism incorporated into each process diagram (Diagrams 1.2 and 1.3).

Work Rule Model

In *Chapters on Machinery and Labor,* Barnett argues that technology determines the demand for process skills and, therefore, determines the level of union employment. Presented in Diagram 1.2, this model's context is to be found in the displacement of handcraftsmen by machines that require a level of skill equal to or less than the skills of the superseded handcraftsman.

The flow of this model begins with the exogenous development of technology and its introduction into printing production. Then, since they are ultimately determined by technology, the demand for process skills determines union employment. New technology might require all, some, or more of the skills of the displaced craftsman. In the case of machine casting, as shown by Barnett, hand compositors often avoided displacement by working as linotype operators. Barnett also cites the usefulness of the displaced bottle-blower's skills in the operation of semiautomatic bottling machines. While much of the skill of the bottle-blowers was not valuable in the operation of the new machinery, machine output was found to vary directly with the skill of the operator. This characteristic led to the employment of displaced bottle-blowers as machine operators.[27]

The availability of union employment opportunities interacts with union wage rates. Together, they determine union responses to technological change. Economic literature assumes that unions will seek to maximize either wages or employment. Theory states that employment varies inversely with the wage rate. Employment is the primary variable because the wage rate for the individual firm is set within fairly narrow limits by competition in the labor market.[28]

Along similar lines, Barnett argues that in shaping union policies, unions desire a high wage rate more than high employment.[29] When choosing between these two competing goals, Hicks explains that trade

DIAGRAM – 1.2. WORK RULE MODEL

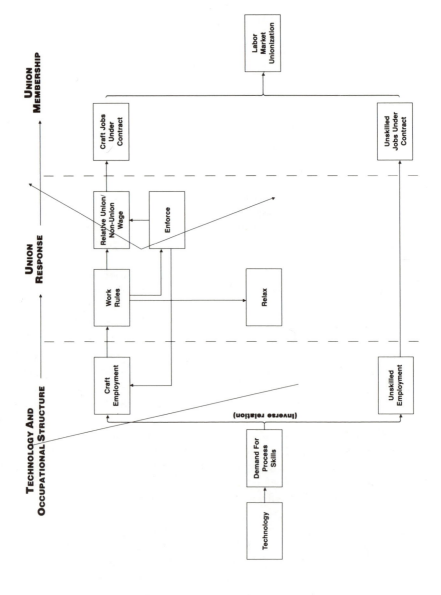

DIAGRAM – 1.3. JOB CONTROL MODEL

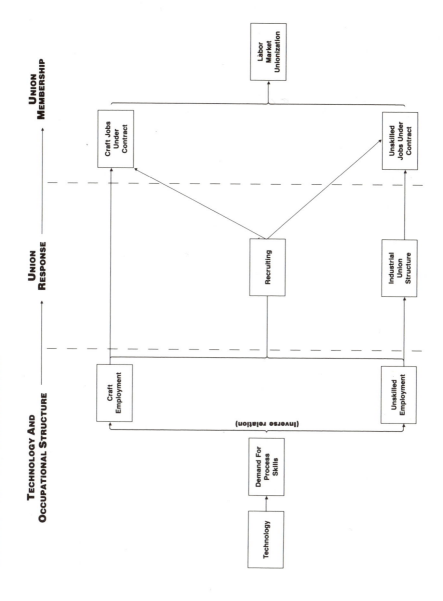

unions customarily choose the apparent good of increased wages over the gradual, obscure employment consequences of wages. He concludes,

> Thus, to the trade unionist, wages and employment naturally appear to have little connection. The initial unemployment may be too small to be really noticeable; and later additions are most easily ascribed to different causes. That which comes from substitution is put down to the "labor-saving machinery"; that which comes from bankruptcy and closing down is ascribed to the inefficiency of employers.[30]

To protect the customary living standards, unions might seek to restrict new process operation to displaced craftsmen. In this respect, the primary work rule printers use to control new process introduction is called the journeyman rule.[31]

This model of craft union response (Diagram 1.2) implies: 1) that the journeyman rule is a consequence of the interaction of union employment and union objectives, and 2) in turn, it also influences the actual introduction of new processes. The model demonstrates that only insofar as the employment of displaced skilled operators leads to the most profitable new process operation will new technology be encouraged in union plants by management. However, a union policy requiring craft workers on jobs that do not require their degree of skill and higher wage will only succeed if the work cannot be done in plants outside union control. Slichter, Healy, and Livernash further argue that the union's effort to compel the payment of the skilled wage in an unskilled process will simply force the work out of the union shop.[32]

Barnett's model fails to consider union policies to compensate for technological displacement, implying a mechanical relation between skill displacement and declining craft union membership. *Chapters on Machinery and Labor* chronicles how defensive union policies, such as those promoting job mobility or offering displaced craftsmen the opportunity to operate new equipment, merely cushion the effects of the introduction of technology upon union membership. While Barnett advocates the organization of unskilled new process workers as a mechanism for counterbalancing skill displacement, this policy is not given sufficient emphasis. He assumes that job opportunities in each union are limited by both inter-union competition and the inability to organize nonunion labor.

Job Control Model

Others suggest that union policies not only retain traditional union functions lost to new process workers—both in and outside of union plants—but can also recapture them. Chandler identifies union restructuring as a policy that maintains union control over existing bargaining unit functions. Munson, Gennard and Dunn identify the strategy of organizing new groups of substitute labor to not only protect union employment, but also to increase it.

The first method to increase union job control is to extend the range of occupational jurisdiction. Chandler argues that a more flexible union structure including both skilled and unskilled new process operators also provides displaced craftsmen greater job mobility. This structure gives the union more power to control the plant labor supply. Chandler also concludes that the merger of individual craft unions into a single industrial union will broaden the range of occupations. Such mergers also limit the impact of particular technologies to a limited portion of the membership.[33]

Without integration, inter-union competition restricts the mobility of the displaced craftsman seeking employment as a cooperant or new process operator, within the trade or within the same occupation but in another industry. Slichter and his co-authors also cite inter-union competition in the rivalry between the letterpress and offset pressmen's unions. In this instance, it is shown how the replacement of letterpress by lithography is an example in which rival union jurisdiction prevented displaced letterpressmen with useful trade skills from operating new offset equipment. The Amalgamated Lithographers of America (ALA) had jurisdiction over the offset process, while the International Printing Pressmen's Union (IPPU) controlled the declining letterpress method. The dispute concerning jurisdiction over the rapidly growing offset branch of the industry ultimately led to the ALA withdrawing from the AFL-CIO in 1945.[34]

Chandler illustrates the importance of a sufficiently broad range of occupational jurisdiction in the cases of the railroad boilermakers and firemen. Both groups were drastically affected by the introduction of the diesel engine. The jurisdiction of the boilermakers was, however, not industry specific. Chandler states that, "The fifty thousand boilermakers who left the railroad shops moved into other fields in construction, shipbuilding and boiler manufacture fields in which the union was active."[35]

Since the boilermaker's jurisdiction is not confined to the railroad industry, the union did not seek to maintain superfluous jobs, through the use of makework rules, for that fraction of its members employed in railroad shops. Displaced boilermakers, by virtue of their lack of industry specificity, could seek employment in other higher-wage industries such as building construction and shipbuilding.[36]

The fireman's situation is quite different. As with typesetters, firemen, as industry operating personnel, could employ their skills only on trains. Since the union is limited to one industry, it cannot aid its membership search for new jobs. Therefore, the firemen use train manning laws and other work rules as their first line of defense in the seemingly unending battle to preserve their craft.[37]

The consolidation of individual craft unions to maintain union jurisdiction over both skilled and unskilled labor assumes the industry boundary as the limit to jurisdiction. Munson, in addition to Gennard and Dunn, take a different approach. They argue that unions should extend their control beyond traditional bargaining units to any location where substitute labor replaces traditional union functions.

Similarly, Stern identifies the problem of an increasing number of competing jobs outside the traditional union bargaining unit.[38] To reestablish control over this new supply of labor, Munson argues that organizing activity is the most important method of securing job rights. In response to the increasing competition of unskilled lithographic industry workers operating the new, simplified equipment, Munson concludes:

> Declining control of the labor supply has meant, in effect, that the union could no longer wait for employers to come to it and ask for help; it had to go out and fight for the right to represent men who produced in competition with organized lithographers, if the job opportunities were to be preserved.[39]

Gennard and Dunn also identify the strategy of organizing the groups of printers spawned by the advent of simplified printing processes in their case study of the one remaining British printing industry craft union, the National Graphical Association (NGA). In 1982, in order to regain control over the printing process, the NGA established a committee to draw up a program for recruiting new members from agencies, studios and from other sources outside the shop floor. This committee studied ways of placing these new members into white collar positions that have replaced the traditional printing and typesetting functions.*

Instead of a mechanical interplay among technology, skill, wages, employment, and union policy, the job control model summarized in Diagram 1.3 suggests that union policies need not be simply passive but can also actively maintain and, in fact, create new job opportunities. Chandler, Munson, and Gennard and Dunn recognize that technology influences union control of job opportunities by altering job skills. For example, the shift from letterpress to lithography transferred jobs from the IPPU to the ALA. In the case of simplified printing processes,

---

* Gennard and Dunn, "The Impact of New Technology," 17, 24–8.

Munson traces the transfer of jobs from skilled members of the ALA to unskilled, nonunion operators.

Diagram 1.3 suggests that union employment varies directly with the union's ability to control job opportunities that had been altered by technology. Responding to variations in employment, unions have been shown to adopt policies of restructuring themselves and of recruiting new membership. The union policy of restructuring to include all skilled and unskilled occupations in the industry increases the range of jobs that the union controls, in turn either maintaining or increasing union employment. While restructuring consolidates union control in traditional areas of influence, by organizing new membership, unions expand the number of jobs, and this in turn expands union membership (Diagram 1.3).

SUMMARY

Chapter 1 has established the basis in economic literature of three hypotheses developed from the craft union membership model. Support for this model is contingent upon establishing the links between production technology, occupational skills, proportional craft employment, relative union/nonunion wages, and printing union membership. If the existence of skill-reducing technology is subsequently established, then economic literature implies by definition that skill-reducing processes may lower the skill requirements of remaining craft workers as well as completely displace craftsmen. Thus, it will lower the proportional labor market employment of skilled workers. Given the existence of both partial and complete craft displacement, the test of the membership model further requires evidence of union policies that maintain skilled relative union/nonunion wage rates.

NOTES

1. Eva Muller, *Technological Advance in an Expanding Economy* (Ann Arbor, MI: University of Michigan Press, 1969), 4 (hereafter cited as *Technological Advance*); and Union Employers of America. "The Future—People and Technology," Special Study Series (Arlington, VA: Printing Industries of America, 1983), 9 (hereafter cited as "The Future").

2. Richard A. Beaumont and Ray B. Helfgath, *Management, Automation and People* (New York: Industrial Relations Counselors, 1964), 35 (hereafter cited as *Automation*); and Jack Simich. Telephone interview with the author, 25 August 1983. Simich is Director of Education, Graphic Arts Technical Foundation, Pittsburgh, PA (hereafter cited as 'Simich, 8/25').

3. Robert V. Eagly, *The Structure of Classical Theory* (New York: Oxford University Press, 1974), 14–15 (hereafter cited as *Classical Theory*).

4. Lloyd G. Reynolds, *The Structure of Labor Markets* (New York: Harper & Brothers, 1951), 140 (hereafter cited as *Labor Markets*).

5. Edwin Mansfield, *The Economics of Technological Change* (New York: W.W. Norton, 1968), 138 (hereafter cited as *Technological Change*).

6. Harry Kelber and Carl Schlessinger, *Union Printers and Controlled Automation* (New York: The Free Press, 1967), 170, 277 (hereafter cited as *Controlled Automation*).

7. Theresa F. Rodgers and Natalie S. Friedman, *Printers Face Automation* (Lexington, MA: Lexington Books, 1980), xvii, 3, 103–4 (hereafter cited as *Face Automation*).

8. Andrew Zimbalist, ed., *Case Studies on the Labor Process* (New York: Monthly Review Press, 1979), 105–10 (hereafter cited as *Case Studies*); and Anthony Smith, *Goodbye Gutenberg* (New York: Oxford University Press, 1980), xi, 207–8 (hereafter cited as *Gutenberg*).

9. Baker, *Printing*, 13.

10. Zimbalist, *Case Studies*, 116–17.

11. John Gennard and Steve Dunn, "The Impact of New Technology on the Structure and Organization of Craft Unions in the Printing Industry," *British Journal of Industrial Relations* XXI(1) March 1985, 19 : (hereafter cited as "Impact of New Technology").

12. Charles Barnett, *Chapters on Machinery and Labor,* (Cambridge: Harvard University Press, 1926) 29, 139 (hereafter cited as *Chapters*).

13. Ibid., 116–17.

14. Ibid., 117.

15. Ibid., 138.

16. Alfred Marshall, *Principles of Economics*, vol. 1, 9th (Varium) ed., with annotation by C. W. Guillebaud (London: Macmillan, 1961), vii, 330, 497–8 (hereafter cited as *Principles*).

17. Barnett, *Chapters*, v–vi, 4.

18. Barnett, *Chapters*, 135–6.

19. Barnett, *Chapters,* 117

20. Reynolds, *Labor Markets*, 1.

21. Barnett, *Chapters*, 5, 7, 13.

22. Munson, *Labor Relations*, 234; The importance of skill-based bargaining leverage is also identified by Dunlop and Higgins, as well as Gennard and Dunn. John T. Dunlop and Benjamin Higgins, "Bargaining Power and Market Structure," *The Journal of Political Economy*, L(1): 2–3 (hereafter cited as "Bargaining Power"), and Gennard and Dunn, "Impact of New Technology," 17.

23. Lloyd G. Reynolds, *Labor Economics and Labor Relations*, 8th ed. (Englewood Cliffs, NJ: Prentice-Hall, 1982), 68–71, 74, 77 (hereafter cited as *Labor Economics*).

24. Arnold R. Weber, "Collective Bargaining and the Challenge of Technological Change," in *Industrial Relations: Challenges and Responses*, John G. Crispo ed. (Toronto: University of Toronto Press, 1966), 78–9 (hereafter cited as "Collective Bargaining"); and Charles Mulvey, *The Economic Analysis of Trade Unions* (New York: St. Martin's Press, 1967), 62 (hereafter cited as *Economic Analysis*).

25. Albert Rees, *The Economics of Trade Unions* (Chicago: University of Chicago Press, 1977), 30–5 (hereafter cited as *Trade Unions*).

26. Charles Craypo, "The Decline of Union Bargaining Power," in *New Directions in Labor Economics and Industrial Relations*, Michael J. Carter and William H. Leahy, eds., (Notre Dame, IN: Notre Dame University Press, 1981) 114–15 (hereafter cited as "Bargaining Power").

27. Barnett, *Chapters,* 124, 135–6.

28. Allan W. Cartter, *Theory of Wages and Employment* (1959; reprinted, Westport, CT: Greenwood Press, 1975), 25, 45 (hereafter cited as *Wages and Employment*); John T. Dunlop, *Wage Determination Under Trade Unions* (1944; reprinted, New York: Augustus M. Kelly, 1966), 77 (hereafter cited as *Wage Determination*); and Wallace N. Atherton, *Theory of Union Bargaining Goals* (Princeton, NJ: Princeton University Press, 1977), 6 (hereafter cited as *Bargaining Goals*).

29. Barnett, *Chapters*, 140.

30. J. R. Hicks, *The Theory of Wages* (London: Macmillan, 1935), 184 (hereafter cited as *Wages*).

31. See George Barnett's analysis of the introduction of the linotype. Barnett, *Chapters*, 26.

32. Sumner H. Slichter. James J. Healy and E. Robert Livernash, *The Impact of Collective Bargaining on Management* (Washington, DC: Brookings Institution, 1960). 365–6 (hereafter cited as *Impact*).

33. Margaret K. Chandler, "Craft Bargaining Power," in *Frontier of Collective Bargaining*, ed. John T. Dunlop and Neil W. Chamberlain (New York: Harper & Row, 1967), 53–4, 61–3 (hereafter cited as "Craft Bargaining").

34. Slichter, et al., *Impact*, 357; and Baker, *Printing and Technology*, 434–5.

35. Chandler, "Craft Bargaining," 55.

36. Richard A. Lester, *The Economics of Labor*, 2d ed. (New York: Macmillan, 1964), 382 (hereafter cited as *Labor*).

37. Chandler, "Craft Bargaining," 55–6.

38. James L. Stern, "Automation and/or a New Day in Unionism." *Annals of the American Academy of Political and Social Science* vol. 350 *The Crisis of American Trade Unions* (November 1969): 25–35 (hereafter cited as "New Day").

39. Munson, *Lithographic Industry*, 214–17.

2

Craft Decline Description

INTRODUCTION

Chapters 2 and 3 are companion chapters describing and measuring the influence of printing production technology upon industry craftsmen. This chapter describes the historical transformation from craft production to automated printing production. Chapter 3 then traces the decline in craft training and the demand for craft production accompanying this transformation. The resulting increase in the ability of management to substitute unskilled for craft labor is also measured in this second chapter.

This craft decline hypothesis states that it is printing production automation that has reduced the level of operator skill required. This hypothesis is tested by separately comparing the necessary production skills of compositors, preparation workers, and press workers in 1958 and again in 1982.

Advances in printing production automation are divided between the major and minor skill reducing innovations developed since 1958, identified as photocomposition, photo-direct offset, and electrostatic printing. This chapter also reviews the history, source, and advantages of these three major deskilling production technologies. Additionally, it considers minor innovations when discussing the effect of technology upon each craft.

The consequence of cathode ray tube (CRT) photocomposition upon the compositor's craft is examined by identifying the four skilled typesetting functions and tracing the influence of technology upon each. In subsequent sections, each compositor's function is defined, its execution in traditional hot type and photocomposition reviewed, and the degree of craft skill displacement measured.

In contrast to the single innovation in composition, both major and minor innovations have affected the skill required in preparation and of press craft workers. Thus, the primary influence of both these processes will be considered separately. Finally, minor innovations incorporating automatic control and mechanization of hand operations will be reviewed.

Skill Reducing Properties of Technological Change

Printers may be grouped according to their involvement in one of the four major stages of production. The first stage is composition. Compositor's set and make up type from original manuscript. The second, or preparatory stage, involves the transfer of original textual and illustrative material to the printing medium, that is, a printing plate, used on press. The pressroom stage involves press operators, press assistants, and feeders who mount the image carriers on presses, feed the presses with ink and paper, supervise the quality of the printing being done, and perform routine maintenance on pressroom machinery. The fourth or finishing stage involves bookbinders and bindery workers. These workers bind printed pages into pamphlets and assemble and otherwise prepare printed material for distribution.[1]

Skill, as a job requirement, is defined as the capacity to perform a given task. The level of skill depends upon the complexity and number of tasks required in a particular occupation. Printing craft workers are distinguished by the relative complexity and large number of required occupational skills. Technology is society's knowledge of physical and social phenomena and the application of these principles to production. This study limits its consideration to those new methods of producing printed matter which have altered the skill level of printing production workers since 1958.[2]

The oldest commercial printing process is letterpress. This process carries the image to be printed on a surface raised above the rest of the printing plate. Letterpress image areas are inked and the plate is then pressed against the paper and removed, leaving an ink image on the paper. The second but most widely used process is lithographic printing. This method transfers images from a plane or flat surface wrapped around a drum. This is in contrast to the letterpress technique of transferring images from depressions or elevations on the printing plate.

In lithography, the image area on the plate is chemically treated to accept ink; the non-image area is similarly treated to repel ink. After the plate has been inked, it is pressed against a rubber surface or "blanket" which accepts the image without wearing down the surface of the plate as does the constant contact with paper in letterpress. The blanket is then used to impress images onto the paper in an operation called "offset".[3]

The discussion will be limited to the two processes of letterpress and lithography. Since 1958 conventional lithography has become the dominant commercial printing process. In terms of 1947 total current dollar value added, lithography accounted for only 24 percent and letterpress 76 percent. After about 1970, lithography became the dominant process, and in 1977 produced 69 percent of the commercial printing sold. The minor processes that are not considered in this study—gravure and engraving—combined amount to less than 10 percent of commercial printing value added in 1977.[4] The conversion from letterpress to lithography during the period under study is not considered significant for our discussion since both processes employ the same level of skill. The replacement of letterpress by lithography only affects the skills of the pressman and not of the compositor, preparation worker or bookbinder. In the case of the pressman, process conversion requires the replacement of one set of comparable craft skills for another.

Evidence of the skill level similarity of the lithographic and letterpressman is found in the historical nonunion and union apprenticeship terms as well as expert opinion. Between 1953 and 1982 training for the nonunion pressman in letterpress or lithography was six years. The number of years' training required for a pressman in both processes is also identical in the two union agreements that determined apprenticeship training between 1950 and 1986.[5]

The effects of technological change prior to 1958 were the substitution of one set of craft skills for another and the automation of manual functions. The composing room was first transformed in the 1880s when machine composition displaced hand compositors. However, Barnett states that the "technical character of the linotype ... requires for its most profitable operation the skill of the superseded hand craftsman."[6]

The second major innovation prior to World War II occurred between 1913 and 1933. It was during this period that new methods of automatic press feeding became the industry standard. Baker concludes that the effect of automatic press feeding was to replace the unskilled assistants rather than the pressmen.[7]

However, what most distinguishes the period since 1958 is the often dramatic reduction of skill required in printing production processes. Two general types of technological change directly reduce the production skills required of printing craftsmen. The first type of such change was the introduction of process automatic control. For instance, CRT photocomposition allows the supervision and regulation of hyphenation, justification, and page make-up to be easily controlled by digital computers. These computers manipulate coded text and tabular matter into the form of a composed page. By 1977, at the end of the period under study, there was increasing evidence that automatically controlled devices, particularly those concerned with digital imaging, would soon displace the skills of both the preparation and pressroom worker. In the preparation department, displacement was seen to be due to computer controlled cameras such as the Opti-copy. These devices are able to photograph and properly impose full forms automatically. In the press-room, computerized press consoles "read errors" and automatically correct them.[8]

The second type of change in production technology is the mechanization of hand operations. Camera, platemaking, and press hand skills requiring long training periods to develop have been displaced by auto-mated equipment.[9]

In addition, technology has created two new methods of printing that displace altogether the skills of the printing craftsman. These methods—photo-direct offset and electrostatic printing—enable unskilled operators to perform what were once craft—and thus union—functions.

Major Skill Reducing Processes

Since this study is concerned with the decline of union membership, consideration is limited to those production processes commercially introduced after 1958 in competition with traditional craft production processes. These three major skill reducing innovations (listed in Table 2.1) are electrophotography, photo direct offset, and digital CRT (cathode ray tube) composition. Each of the three major innovations enables automatic process control to displace craft production methods. Each innovation, including its definition, history and source, and advantages, are covered below.

Table 2.1: Major Skill-Reducing Printing Processes, 1958–83

Function and Process	Commercial Introduction
Press: Electrophotography	1959
Preparation and Press: Photo-Direct Offset (Copy-to-Plate)	1963
Composition: Digital CRT (Cathode Ray Tube) Typesetter	1967

Source: Compiled by the author.

The technological change producing these three major skill reducing innovations is shown in this chapter to have come from outside the printing industry. RCA developed and shipped the first CRT photocomposition equipment in 1967. Earlier versions of photocomposition devices were developed by such nonprinting companies as American Type Founders, Mergenthaler, and Singer. The photo-direct method depended, in turn, on the innovations of A. B. Dick, Eastman-Kodak, and Itek. Electrostatic printing was originally developed by Xerox.

This study's hypothesis that technology has reduced the level of operator skill required in production is tested separately by comparing the necessary skills of the compositor, preparation and press workers between 1958 and the date of the new production processes. CRT photocomposition is shown in this chapter to have automated three of the four skilled functions of the typesetter's craft. This equipment automatically hyphenates, justifies, and largely eliminates the need for make-up because of the instructions governing repetitive formats stored in computer memory. The fourth skill, proofreading, is seen not to have been affected by photocomposition.

The late James E. Horne, an acknowledged authority on industrial relations in the printing industry, states that the range of operations requiring craft skills were halved with the displacement of hot type with photocomposition typesetting methods. Confirming Horne's estimate, NCA data indicate that craft skills are only required in 31 percent of sampled photocomposition production hours. Photocomposition only requires craft skills in mark-up and proofreading. As a percentage of total production hours on NCA standard pages, mark-up required 8 percent and proofreading 23 percent of the production hours of members surveyed. The balance of photocomposition production functions require no more skill than that needed of an office typist.

The major innovations of photo-direct offset and electrostatic printing completely displaced the demand for preparation and press craft skills. Copy-to-plate printing requires the operation of the Itek combination camera/platemaker and small press equipment similar to the A. B. Dick press. Instead of a preparation craftsman, the Itek platemaker can be operated by an unskilled worker after less than one day's training. An A. B. Dick Company representative states that operator training on their press required only three days' training in 1955 and only one day in 1978. Xerox indicates that operator training on large copier/duplicator models declined from 16 to 10 hours between 1974 and 1983. Equipment manufacturers' statements all indicate that the photo-direct and electrostatic printing processes reduced the preparation and press craft functions to the level of those required of an unskilled operator for single-color, short-run press work within the capabilities of these new processes.

Six minor innovations reduced the level of manual preparation and press craft skills. Automatic development and exposure equipment, together with presensitized plate material, reduced the hand skills required of the preparation craft worker. Electronic press controls, registration systems, and the automatic balancing of ink and water fountain solutions reduced the demand for craft skills in the pressroom.

As technology replaces antiquated and manually controlled printing equipment, printers are losing their distinctive craft or industry specific skills. Computer input, operation and proofreading are functions now common to commercial data processing installations. Photodirect and electrostatic printing equipment operate in modern office environments with unskilled operators. On larger, complicated printing equipment, printers require a more general knowledge common to operators of other electronically controlled production machinery.

CRT PHOTOCOMPOSITION

Definition

The introduction of photocomposition has been described as the third major development, following movable type and hot metal casting, to change the structure of the printing industry. Photocomposition involves the transfer of optical characters from a negative master onto a photographic emulsion. Provision must be made for proper illumination, image formation, magnification or reduction, and positioning of each image. Typographic quality output is achieved in photocomposition by automatic selection from among relatively large sets of characters, by controlled positioning, and by the insertion of special symbols and characters.[10]

Many techniques and configurations of mechanical, optical, and electronic equipment are used in photocomposition. CRT typesetters are the major photocomposition innovation because they have displaced the skilled compositors who previously performed make-up and setting functions.

History and Source

The development of CRT typesetters is set within the context of the relationship between typesetting and data processing. Of course, any computer manipulation in typesetting, such as hyphenation, justification, or pagination, is a form of data processing.[11] Simplistically, one may consider second or third generation typesetters to be further developments of the common computer line printer. The development of photocomposition has depended to a large extent upon the simultaneous enhancement of typesetting qualities of computer generated output.

The development of each photocomposition generation permitted setting an ever-expanding range of copy. The first generation was used to typeset copy of relatively standard format, type style, and size. The second and third generations of typesetting were successively able to set copy that required greater variability in format, style, and size. The standard format permitted large dailies to be the first segment of the printing industry to use digital computers as production tools. By 1964, computers for newspaper typesetting had already become commonplace. The application of photocomposition to advertising and book copy was, however, still in its infancy.[12]

In terms of delivery, expert opinion sets 1967 as the date of the first commercialization of CRT typesetters. Notable industry experts on modern photocomposition, in independent interviews, agree that the first commercialization of the third generation CRT typesetters began with the introduction of the RCA Video Comp. RCA began shipping Model 820 CRT typesetting devices in 1967.[13]

The development of photocomposition came from outside the printing industry and through the support of large corporate and government consumers. Photocomposition devices were not invented, manufactured, or marketed by commercial printers.

Seybold marks 1946 as the beginning of the era of photocomposition. In 1946, the Intertype Foto-typesetter was field tested and an agreement concluded between Lithomat Company and two Frenchmen, Rene Higonnet and Louis Meyroud, which led to the development of the phototypesetter. With development fully underway toward the conclusion of World War II, the first Fotosetter units were tested in the U.S. Government Printing Office as early as 1946. The first generation Intertype Fotosetter unit was exhibited in 1950. The other first generation phototypesetter, the Monophoto, was originally developed by British Monotype's George Westover as the Rotophoto in 1949. It subsequently emerged in 1955 as the Monophoto.[14]

The first second-generation typesetter was the Photon 200. This machine was initially developed in the 1940s. It was brought to the United States by its inventors, Meyroud and Higonnet, while still in the conceptional stage. The Photon was initially conceived as a quasi-nonprofit venture, and financing for it was sought from influential backers in the printing and publishing industry. After the initial infusion of capital, it was restructured as a publicly held corporation.[15]

This RCA Video Comp was the first of the third generation CRT typesetters. This machine was developed by Dr. Ing. Rudolf Hill, an electronic component and device manufacturer in Kiel, West Germany. Seybold reports that in 1964 Dr. Hill was approached by parties interested in determining whether or not he could produce a device able to compose telephone directory galleys on 70mm. film. This initial contact led to discussions with other customers. It was during these explorations that the concept of the Digiset 50 T1 emerged. Subsequently, this machine was sold in the United States as the Video Comp 820. After a 1966 visit to the United States by Dr. Hill, an arrangement was made with RCA to market the Video Comp.[16]

The first generation of phototypesetters adapted raised hot metal casting to set type and compose copy. The second generation machines were specially conceived and designed to set type by photographic means. The third generation typesetter does not expose type directly to photographic masters but rather reproduces them electronically on the face of a cathode ray tube, a device similar to a TV screen. The images thus created are photographed directly from the face of the machine.[17]

Seybold defines a third generation CRT typesetter as one which:

> a) generates characters on the face of a CRT as strokes or dot patterns; b) accepts input primarily from a computer rather than directly from a keyboard; c) operates at high speeds in excess of several hundred characters per second; and d) is frequently used to output fully-composed pages of type (as opposed to galleys).[18]

Seybold classifies CRT typesetters into two categories, depending upon the method of character storage. One category creates a character image on the face of the CRT by simultaneously scanning a photographic master. Hence, the "character store" is considered photographic even though the image is not exposed on film by the conventional means of shining a light through it. Instead, the information derived from scanning this photographic master is converted into analog signals. These, in turn, instruct the deflection circuitry of the CRT where and how to draw or paint the output character.[19]

The alternative approach is to store the characters as a digital representation instead of as photographic images. Once the digital representation of each character or image is stored in memory, it can be retrieved, duplicated, and re-used by many different remotely-located typesetters whenever that character is desired.[20]

Advantages

The major advantages of photocomposition are image quality and reduced unit cost. Since World War II, there has been a shift in the printing process from letterpress to offset methods. While letterpress requires printing from a raised surface, offset lithography requires exposure of the plate to a photographic negative or positive. The use of raised type for offset printing requires a series of elaborate and costly conversion techniques providing an equivalent of a photographic positive from metal.[21] Quality suffers as a result since positive type images are susceptible to irregular impressions due to unevenly worn type and character castings.

The demand for photocomposition increased in direct proportion to the popularity of lithography. In 1947, offset accounted for 24 percent and letterpress for 76 percent of total commercial printing value added. By about 1970 offset lithography became the dominant process, and by 1977 it produced 69 percent of all commercial printing sold.[22]

Photocomposition economies emanate from the saving of original keystrokes and the elimination of make-up decisions and coding through the use of repetitive formats. In a 1982 survey of 166 firms, the National Association of Printers and Lithographers concluded that 40 percent of all copy is directly transmitted to the printer or word processing media in this manner. As a consequence, the customer eliminates the need for repetitious keystrokes. Additionally, customers supplying manuscripts in machine readable form also realize faster turnaround, increased accuracy, a reduction in proofreading requirements, and lower typesetting costs.[23] Telephone directories are an ideal application for photocomposition. Instead of original keystroking, customer names and addresses are abstracted from telephone company computerized accounting files. Detailed coding of each page's make-up specification is replaced with a simple terminal instruction to repeat a repetitive page format.

Representative CRT photocomposition unit cost data are not available due to the wide variety of CRT capabilities and costs. However, an attempt will be made here to estimate the range of unit cost savings attributable to third generation photocomposition.

The Porte Publishing Company's *Franklin Offset Catalog* lists appropriate comparative unit cost data for both photocomposition and type processes. Starting with 1977 these annual unit cost data include all direct and indirect expenses derived from a national survey of printers. A comparable 8½ x 11″ page of text matter of medium quality is used as the unit of measure. Table 2.2 summarizes the comparative unit costs and indicates that photocomposition cost ranges between 2 percent and 5 percent less than hot type processes.

Unfortunately, Porte data assume more primitive first and second generation equipment as indicated by the hourly cost rates listed in the

Table 2.2: **Photo and Hot Composition Unit Cost Comparison 1977–83** *(page rate)*

Year	Photo Composition $	Hot Type Composition $	Photo to Hot Composition (Present) Ratio
1977	26.70	28.10	.95
1978	29.79	30.47	.98
1979	32.28	33.03	.98
1980	36.37	37.23	.98
1981	41.16	42.44	.97
1982	45.25	47.21	.96
1983	48.10	50.40	.95

Source: Compiled by the author.

catalog. Most important, the *Franklin* data ignored the two most significant economies of photocomposition: keystroke savings and repetitive formats.[24]

John W. Seybold has stated that the chief advantage of CRT photocomposition is that it increases labor productivity from a low of 2-to-1 in financial matter to a high of 100-to-1 in directory matter. This latter application takes advantage of the CRT typesetter's ability to manipulate data bases electronically and thus save keystrokes and repetitive decision making.[25]

PHOTO-DIRECT OFFSET

Definition

Photo-direct offset is a lithographic process that permits printing on simplified presses without the need for negatives. The distinguishing feature of the photo-direct method is its use of presensitized paper plate material, direct plate exposure, and the simplified press balancing of water and ink required in this process. Because of this feature, photo-direct offset is sometimes referred to as the copy-to-plate method. It differs from traditional lithographic platemaking in that it does not require the use of an intermediate imposed negative. Moreover, traditional press operation requires the skillful balancing of the ink and water fountain solutions. This is not a requirement in the copy-to-plate method.

History and Source

Technological change has been shown to have come from outside the printing industry. The *Kodak Graphic Arts Manpower Survey* states that this situation will continue with spectacular breakthroughs in optics, chemistry, plastics and electronics, fluidics and other technologies. Progress in these areas will continue to be absorbed by the printing industry.[26]

Photo-direct printing became a viable alternative to the craftsmen's more complicated and conventional lithography after the combination of three independent innovations.

The first firm to develop the copy-to-plate process was the A. B. Dick Company. In July 1955, A. B. Dick shipped its first Model 350 Offset Press. The principal advantage of this press is its dampening system which allows a more rapid balancing of water and ink. This system also permits a more rapid set-up when shifting between standard paper sizes and stocks. This press carries water on top of the ink instead of using the conventional dampening system. Prior to the A. B. Dick Company innovations, the dampening unit kept non-image areas of the plate receptive to water and repellent to ink.[27]

The year 1961 marks Eastman-Kodak's successful commercialization of its then recently developed projection plate material. The demand for this new plate material started to increase after the development of the Itek camera-platemaker.[28]

The primary advantage of this projection plate is that it is presensitized and thereby avoids complicated chemical treatment before and after exposure. As a direct result of this, the plate material can simply be taken from the manufacturer's original container and immediately exposed to the customer copy. In this way plates can be made in less than two minutes and without the need for either a darkroom or more than a few hours' training. These plates produce high quality line work and acceptable halftones.[29]

Kodak contacted Itek in the hope that they would be able to develop a combination camera/platemaker built around the new Kodak project-a-lith plate material. Itek shipped the first of these camera/platemakers in 1962. This equipment integrated the previously separate functions of camera stripping and platemaking. This platemaker exposes the printing plate directly to customer copy. First, the customer copy is placed in front of the camera lens, then, by pressing a button, a paper plate is automatically exposed, developed, and stabilized. The plate material usually comes on a roll which is automatically cut to size. This, in turn, is carried through the processing solutions by a series of rollers and belts.[30]

Commercialized in 1962, the Itek platemaker was the last of the three photo-direct offset process innovations. The combination of all three innovations enabled this process to become a viable alternative in short-run commercial printing.[31] Though presently expanding, the technical capabilities of the process generally limit camera direct work in terms of run length and quality. Jobs consisting of less than 5,000 impressions of single-color line work are usually printed using this process. Color printing or fine photographic reproduction are presently beyond the capabilities of this process.

Advantages

The major advantage of photo-direct over traditional offset is the lower unit cost in quantities of less than 1,000 sheets. Unit cost data indicate that this method is 45 to 50 percent less expensive than traditional offset in quantities of 100 copies. The labor and materials needed to make photo-direct paper plates are less time consuming and expensive than conventional metal plates. These lower fixed labor and material costs in each press run are the cause of reduced photo-direct unit costs.

However, though conventional metal plates cost more, they produce two to three times more impressions. These longer-life metal plates allow lower conventional offset unit costs in quantities over 1,000 sheets. As production runs exceed 1,000 sheets, set-up time for each worn out paper plate and the cost of replacement of photo-direct plates on the slower press cause the relative unit cost of conventional offset to decrease.

Table 2.3 summarizes relative unit costs for both conventional and photo-direct methods. Neither Porte nor Prudential Publishing Companies have cost data for all three processes of conventional offset, electrostatic, and photo-direct printing. Porte conventional costs are compared with electrostatic and photo-direct unit costs available only from Prudential Publishing Company. Porte conventional unit cost data include all direct and indirect expenses based upon a national printers survey. Conventional process costs include only labor and overhead for manually processed line plates and press work, and exclude identical material costs, particularly paper. Porte's category of "ordinary" or poor quality is used because it includes the single-color, nonregister-type work within the capability of photo-direct methods. Ordinary offset includes coarse lines, drawings, and halftones. Paper and bindery costs are not affected by the choice of either conventional or photo-direct processes.[32] To allow comparison of Porte and Prudential data, the common unit of

Table 2.3:   Photo-Direct and Conventional Offset Process Unit Cost Comparison, 1976–83

Year	Photo-Direct/Conventional Process Unit Cost	
	100 Copies	1000 Copies
1976	.61	1.16
1977	.62	1.33
1978	.59	1.40
1979	.57	1.49
1980	.55	1.52
1981	.53	1.53
1982	.52	1.55
1983	.50	1.54

Source: Compiled by the author.

measure is an $8\frac{1}{2}$ x 11″ sheet of cut paper, printed on one side with black ink and of ordinary quality.

Prudential photo-direct unit cost data also include both direct and indirect costs (compiled on the basis of the author's experience and a national survey of printing plants), but exclude the cost of paper. Conventional offset method data are not available from Prudential Publishing.[33]

The unit cost data summarized in Table 2.3 indicate that the relative cost of photo-direct printing has decreased in the smaller quantities of 1,000 sheets due to lower, fixed plate cost. Given that metal and paper plates utilize the same press equipment,[34] the increasing competitiveness of the photo-direct process in smaller quantities is due to decreasing relative labor and materials costs of paper plates.

ELECTROSTATIC PRINTING

Definition

Electrostatic printing utilizes corona from high voltages. This corona is applied to needles or nibs to produce shaped electrostatic charges on paper. In contrast to conventional and photo-direct offset, electrostatic printers do not use plates. All electrostatic printers are image carriers that transfer an image to paper. The image is replaced after every impression.[35]

History and Source

Electrostatic printing on plain paper began on October 22, 1938 with the invention of xerography by Chester Carlson. The early history of electrostatic printing is almost synonymous with the development of xerography. In 1949, the first copier, "Xerox X," was introduced. This copier was slow and required a number of carefully executed manual operations to produce a decent copy. The major application of the Xerox X copier was to produce quick masters for a type of small office printing press requiring paper masters that were, at that time, primarily typed by hand. In 1955 came Copy Flo. This was the first completely automated xerographic machine. It produced enlarged prints on continuous rolls of microfilm originals.

In 1959, Xerox introduced the Model 914, a fast, cheap, and convenient office copier. By the end of 1962, 10,000 Model 914 copiers had been shipped. Xerox states that the Model 914 "launched a major corporation and revolutionized an industry." The Xerox 914 provided a floor model copier producing seven copies per minute. It was the first office copier to make copies on ordinary paper.[36]

Advantages

Electrostatic printing offers no advantages for large volume production, but for copying it has the major advantages producing an image on paper so inexpensively that the plate can be disposed of after each copy. Comparative unit cost data are not available from Xerox because the company considers these data to be of a proprietary nature.[37]

Electrostatic unit costs are available from both Prudential Publishing and the Canadian Government's Department of Supply and Services (DDS). These unit costs are summarized in Table 2.4. Prudential data indicate that, in quantities of 100, electrostatic printing costs have ranged between 24 and 28 percent of conventional offset costs since 1976. Neither Porte nor Prudential Publishing Companies have cost data for all three processes of conventional offset, electrostatic and photo-direct printing. Porte conventional costs are compared with electrostatic and photo-direct unit costs which are only available from Prudential Publishing Company.

Table 2.4 shows that quantities over 1,000 are still most economically printed by conventional offset. Cost data for smaller quantities are divided between copy-to-plate and electrostatic printing. As a rule of thumb, the National Association of Printers and Lithographers reports that 50 copies or less are best produced on electrostatic equipment.[38] For quantities of over 50 copies but less than 1,000, photo-direct is usually the most efficient method, as is indicated in Table 2.4.

The Canadian Government's *Equipment Utilization Guide* indicates that electrostatic printing is used when producing up to 30 one

Table 2.4: Electrostatic and Conventional Process Unit Cost Comparison, 1976–83

| | Electrostatic/Conventional Process Cost | |
Year	100 Copies	1000 Copies
1976	.34	2.44
1977	.34	2.46
1978	.32	2.36
1979	.31	2.30
1980	.30	2.20
1981	.29	2.09
1982	.28	2.02
1983	.28	1.96
Canadian Government Data		
1978		1.96

Source: Compiled by the author.

sided originals. Photo-direct duplication should be used when over 100 copies are required. Published unit cost data indicate that electrostatic unit costs rise to 95 percent of photo-direct unit costs in quantities of 100.[39]

Electrostatic technology also offers the added advantages of being able to be conveniently located within office environments and of being linked to a computer. Digitally stored information can be updated, accessed, and distributed through electrostatic printers linked to a main frame computer.[40] With the increasing capability of electrostatic color and halftone reproduction, the nonconventional printing process is likely to further replace traditional printing methods.

TECHNOLOGY'S IMPACT UPON PRINTING CRAFTS

In order to link technological change and occupational skill, the subsequent section will describe the number and complexity of skills required by industry craftsmen before and after new process introduction.

Typesetting

The consequence of CRT photocomposition upon the typesetter's craft is examined here by identifying the four major skilled printing functions and tracing the influence of technology upon each. In subsequent sections, each compositor's function will be defined, its execution in traditional hot type and photocomposition reviewed, and the degree of skill displacement measured. A Department of Commerce review of 1967 outlined the influence of digital composition upon the compositor's craft as follows:

> The computer, then in one of its many roles, has been gradually and painstakingly assuming an increasingly important position as skilled compositor, to which it is rather ideally suited, since this task involves an enormous repetition of well-defined decision processes. The computer has already demonstrated its ability to eliminate the need for the complex compositor skills from the keyboard operator, to provide an enormous increase in the speed of the compositor functions, and to keep pace with developments in electronic photocomposers which promise typesetting of graphic arts quality at speed of thousands of characters per second, intermixed with electronically photocomposed line art, screened halftones, and continuous tone illustrations.[41]

The four primary functions of a compositor's craft are justification, hyphenation, make-up, and proofreading. Each of the four composition functions requires a high level of skill. Justification entails deciding where to end a line of type so that it remains within predetermined margins. Hyphenation is deciding where and when to hyphenate words that would exceed the margin.[42] By make-up is meant the assembling of all lines of type in proper sequence and style. During the proofreading function, copy is checked for errors and any changes are marked for correction.

Since the turn of the century until about 1970, most composition in the United States was produced by hot type line casting machines. Hot metal typecasting equipment begins with matrices which are either correctly assembled or positioned for the casting of type. Different matrices correspond to each character, type face, and point size. Each matrix serves as the bottom of the casting mold where it is positioned with its intaglio cavity facing up. The caster pours the hot molten type metal into the mold to cast one line of type. The matrices of a specific type face and size are housed within a magazine. Each time copy requires a different type face or print size, the operator lifts and moves a 50- to 70-pound magazine by hand.[43]

Tracing the flow of copy through composition will help identify both relative skill and labor requirements of hot and photocomposition processes. Manuscript is received in the composing room where it is "copy cut" according to the type faces, sizes, and measures of type to be composed.[44] In hot type, the operator of the linecaster uses the machine keyboard to cast each line or "slug" separately into long galleys.

The journeyman typesetting operator performs the functions of hyphenation and justification. Proofs are usually pulled by an apprentice. Each galley is identified by number and the type is laid out sequentially. Hand compositors or "bank men" make up the pages from separately cast galleys of footnotes, text, and display matter. Once all the typographical ingredients—type, tabular, display, and footnotes—are assembled, new pages, proofs, are pulled for the proofreaders. Dividing galleys into pages, inserting headings, folios, positioning illustrations, mixing type faces and line lengths are all done by hand compositors in make-up. After the customer has approved the proofs, the compositor paginates and imposes the pages into forms for press.

The only one of four skilled typesetting functions not affected by photocomposition is proofreading. The use of photocomposition meant that the remaining typesetting activities required less skill. Mark-up or copy cutting is required less often since computer compositors store repetitive formats that can be recalled upon command. For example, by retrieving a particular stored format, the input operator does not have to specify type face, point size of text, heading, or the indentation of paragraph beginnings or page folios. In the case of hot type, the operator might remember a repetitive format but would have to replicate each instruction on his keyboard for each galley set.

In photocomposition, the remaining operator functions require less skill. CRT photocomposition devices automatically hyphenate and justify on the basis of stored instructions. In hot metal, the operator would make a decision regarding line "breaks" at the end of each line cast as well as when and where to hyphenate. In photocomposition, however, the input operator only keyboards the copy along with marked up typographic coding. In contrast to hot type, changes in type faces and point size are executed by the computer following coded commands.

Photocomposition reduces, if not eliminates, the need for hand page make-up. Depending upon the particular system, keyboard codes instruct the central processing unit on how to compose each page. In hot type, each line is found, cut, cleaned, and assembled by hand. A comparatively simple column for an $8\frac{1}{2}$ x 11″ page of straight text matter has 50 lines or slugs.

Expert opinion and trade literature suggest that photocomposition significantly reduces the amount of typesetting craft production skills require. Horne estimates that during the 1970s the degree of skilled typesetting functions more than halved with the introduction of photocomposition. According to Horne, 70 percent of the operations in commercial, hot typesetting were skilled, while only 30 percent of the operations in photocomposition were skilled.[45]

Confirming Horne's estimate, National Composition Association (NCA) data indicate that craft skills are only required in 31 percent of photocomposition production hours. Photocomposition requires craft skills only in make-up and proofreading. As percent of total production hours on NCA standard pages, mark-up required 8 percent and proofreading 23 percent of members surveyed. The balance of photo-composition production functions require no more skill than that of an office typist.[46]

Preparation

In lithographic processes, copy preparation requires the three highly-skilled functions of photography, stripping, and platemaking. An apprentice in the preparation department is trained in all three skilled functions before specializing.

Photography's objective is the conversion of original images into transparent intermediaries for platemaking. Offset lithography requires that original positive copy is converted into a negative image so that in the process transfer from cylinder to print image the copy is converted back into its original positive, readable form. The cameraman determines the appropriate exposure, film, screen value, and development of the transparent intermediary for each piece of customer copy. Line and halftone photography record original images in a manner making it possible to convert them into printing page carriers. Photographs require an intermediate screen that converts continuous tone images into a pattern of exceedingly small and clearly defined dots of controlled size. Once exposed, the film is developed and stabilized by the cameraman.[47]

The next step is called stripping. If the finished page is to include a picture and text, the transparent negative must be precisely positioned prior to making the plate. Printing in more than one color adds considerable complexity to the stripping operation. When printing one color, units of copy must be assembled for exposure on a single plate. Multicolor printing requires different plates for each color. These are registered in such a way as to overprint each other precisely.[48]

The purpose of the stripping function is to convert the original photographed text and art into image carriers for offset lithography. Strippers perform six main tasks that require manual skill and judgment. The craftsman plans the press plate contacts; performs tinting, laying, ruling, scribing, and retouching tasks; prepares for the stripping support medium; adapts and fits photographic intermediaries for assembly; and completes the assembly of the stripped flat.

Platemaking is the final phase in conversion of original images into offset printing image carriers. The product of lithographic platemaking is a single unit image carrier. All images on the carrier are completely assembled as they will appear on the printed sheet.[49] Platemaking involves three steps: preparing the plate to receive the image, placing the image on the plate, and developing the exposed image.

In the first step, the platemaker begins with a plate surface photo-mechanical coating. Depending on the type of plate, the surface is sensitized by rubbing the area to be exposed with chemical solutions. The complete transparent image carrier is then laid on top of the sensitized plate surface and exposed to a bright light. After exposure on a vacuum frame, the non-image areas are removed during development. The uniformity of image required of even single-color, continuous-tone printing makes high precision plates an absolute necessity. Strauss illustrated the need for precision:

> In 133-line halftones, which are commonly used in the reproduction of black-and-white photographs, each square inch consists of almost 18,000 individual units. Practically each of these 18,000 units is further divided into a printing and non-printing area and the proportion of these two kinds of areas varies for different tones, or values, of the picture. Dividing a lithographic plate into printing and non-printing areas of such minute sizes, and, consequently of an enormous number of such divisions is quite an undertaking. Nor should the difficulty of keeping such a plate in perfect state during presswork be underestimated.[50]

Within the preparation workers' craft, technology has impacted skills through a series of minor as well as two major innovations. Four new types of production equipment incorporating automatic control and the automation of hand operations have reduced the level of craft skill. The major innovations of photo-direct offset and electrostatic printing completely displaced the demand for preparation craft skills.

In 1958, the graphic arts camera function required both theoretical knowledge and manual dexterity to expose and develop copy images. In addition, an adequate understanding of each lens and its exposure requirements necessitated an understanding of both physics and optics. An understanding of photographic materials and processing methods, in turn, required a knowledge of chemistry. By the late 1960s, however, automated camera exposure meters and film processing devices were introduced. Log E commercialized the first automatic film developer in 1964. As a consequence of this combination of automatic exposure and developing, both the technical knowledge and manual skills required in camera work were reduced.[51]

Two other developments have simplified platemaking: presensitized plates and automatic plate developing. Presensitized plates simplified platemaking by removing the required application of a chemical coating on the raw plate prior to exposure. Since 1950, presensitized plates have gained in popularity and became the norm in the late 1960s.

the large sheetfed installations. Apart from mounting to plate, there is now very little need for the pressmen to work in the press except in emergencies. The setting of fountain keys, filling of the fountain, maintenance of color to color, lateral and print to cut register blanket cleaning, etc. can be either automatic or remotely controlled from the press console.[61]

Image quality and register systems reduce press operator experience requirements. Process control instrumentation, largely from the application of the microcomputer and microprocessor, assist the operator in accomplishing register, coming up to color strength, and in quickly printing the proper tonal reproduction. For example, placing a press sheet under a reflection densitometer gives the pressman a numerical readout of color values. These, when compared to standards or customer copy, indicate specific press adjustments.[62] Prior to the use of the densitometer, color and total adjustments were based upon the intuitive decisions of craftsmen.

While automatic dampening and register systems only reduced the level of press skills, copy-to-plate and electrostatic equipment reduced printing to an unskilled operation. Equipment manufacturers indicated that copy-to-plate and electrostatic machinery require only an unskilled operator. Photo-direct press operation required three days of training in 1955 and one day of training in 1978.[63]

Xerox, the major manufacturer of electrostatic printers, indicated that operator training of the large volume Model 9200 was approximately 16 hours in 1974 and that this has been reduced to only about 10 hours in 1983. Smaller Xerox models used as substitutes for the printing press require even less training. For example, the Xerox 2400, the first copier/duplicator, originally required 3 hours of training in 1964. By 1983, only approximately 2 training hours were required. Joseph Scheldrick, an industry expert, also suggests that a few hours training for each operator is adequate.[64]

SUMMARY

Chapter 2 describes the techniques that are transforming the printing process from craft to lesser skilled and unskilled automated production. Technological change has taken the form of automatic process control and mechanization of hand operations.

Chapter 2 established that photocomposition and other minor innovations have reduced the number and complexity of typesetting, preparation and press craft skills, and has also described how photo-direct offset and electrophotography have completely displaced the crafts of preparation and press workers in the production of single-color printed matter.

NOTES

1. Bureau of Labor Statistics. U.S. Department of Commerce. *Union Wages and Benefits: Printing Trades*, bulletin 2049 (Washington, DC: GPO, 1978), 1 (hereafter cited as *Union Wages*).

2. Robert Max Jackson, *The Formation of Craft Labor Markets* (Orlando: Academic Press, 1984) 27, 261. (hereinafter Cited as *Formation*); and Edwin Mansfield, *Microeconomics*, (New York: W. W. Norton, 1970) 10, 441–6.

3. Bureau of Labor Statistics. U.S. Department of Labor. *Union Wages.*

4. U.S. Department of Commerce. Bureau of the Census. *1977 Census of Manufacturers* (Washington, DC: GPO, 1980), 106–9 (hereafter cited as *1977 Manufacturers.*)

5. "Recommended Standards of Wages and Hours" approved by the Master Printers Section of the Printing Industries of Metropolitan New York, Inc., 1958–82; "Standards of Apprenticeship for Pressmen," by the Joint Negotiating Committee of the Printers' League Section, New York Employing Printers Association and New York Printing Pressmen's Union No. 51, May 24, 1950 and amended April 1, 1953; "Contract for Book and Job Shops between Printers' League Section, Printing Industries of Metropolitan New York, Inc. and New York Printing Pressmen and Offset Workers' Union No. 51" for the period 1971–74, 28–32; "Contract for Book and Job Shops between Printers' League Section, Printing Industries of Metropolitan New York and the Printing and Graphic Communications Union No. 51" for the period 1983–86, 64–7; James E. Horne. Telephone interview with the author, 11 April 1983. Mr. Horne is executive vice-president, Printers' League Section, Printing Industries of Metropolitan New York. Horne serves as employer-negotiator for this group (hereafter cited as Horne 4/11); and Jack Simich. Telephone interview with the author, 21 March 1983 (hereafter cited as Simich, 3/21).

6. Charles Barnett, *Chapters on Machinery and Labor,* (Cambridge: Harvard University Press, 1926) 29 (hereafter cited as *Chapters*).

7. Elizabeth Faulkner Baker, *Printers and Technology: A History of the International Printing Pressmen and Assistants Union,* (New York: Columbia University Press, 1957), 215 (hereafter cited as *Printing).*

8. Eva Muller, *Technological Advance in an Expanding Economy* (Ann Arbor, MI: University of Michigan Press, 1969) 4 (hereafter cited as *Technological Advance*); and Union Employers of America. "The Future—People and Technology," Special Study

Series (Arlington, VA: Printing Industries of America, 1983) 9 (hereafter cited as "The Future").

9.   Richard A. Beaumont and Ray B. Helfgath, *Management, Automation and People* (New York: Industrial Relations Counsellors, 1964), 35 (hereafter cited as *Automation*); and Jack Simich. Telephone interview with the author, 25 August 1983. (hereafter cited as Simich 8/25).

10.   U.S. Department of Commerce. National Bureau of Standards. *Automatic Typographic Quality Typesetting Techniques: A State of the Art Review,* monograph 99, (Washington, DC: GPO, 1967), 21–2 (hereafter cited as *Quality Typesetting*).

11.   John W. Seybold, *Fundamentals of Modern Photocomposition* (Media, PA: Seybold Publications, 1979), 368 (hereafter cited as *Modern Photocomposition*).

12.   Victor Strauss, *The Printing Industry* (Arlington, VA: Printing Industries of America, 1967) 123 (hereafter cited as *Printing*), and U.S. Department of Commerce. Bureau of Domestic Commerce. *Printing and Publishing.* (Washington, DC: Superintendent of Documents, January, 1965) pp. 6–7.

13.   Frank J. Romano. Telephone interview with the author, 15 September 1983. Romano is editor and publisher of *New England Printer and Publisher* (hereafter cited as Romano 9/15); John W. Seybold. Telephone interview with the author 16 September 1983 (hereafter cited as Seybold 9/16); and Seybold, *Modern Photocomposition,* 139.

14.   Seybold, *Modern Photocomposition,* 78–9.

15.   Ibid., 79.

16.   Ibid., 139.

17.   Ibid., 1–2, 119.

18.   Ibid., 120.

19.   Ibid., 119.

20.   Ibid., 120, 135.

21.   Ibid., 7.

22.   U.S. Department of Commerce. *1977 Manufacturers,* 27 C–7.

23.   National Association of Printers and Lithographers, *Word Processing's Impact of Today's Typesetting* (Teaneck, NJ: The Association, 1982) 1–6 (hereafter cited as *Today's Typesetting*).

24.   Porte Publishing Company, "Hour Rates, Negatives, Flats, Plates, Presswork, Photo Composition, etc.," in *Franklin Offset Catalog, Section D* (Salt Lake City, UT: Porte Publishing, July 1983), 3 (hereafter cited as *Franklin*); and Elman Snow. Personal correspondence with the author, 9 January 1984. Snow is president, Porte Publishing Company.

25.   Seybold 9/16.

26.   Eastman-Kodak Company. *Manpower,* 3.

27.   Donald Daniels. Telephone interview with the author, 30 September 1983. Daniels is marketing manager, small duplicators for the A. B. Dick Company (hereafter cited as Daniels 9/30); and William Friday, *Quick Printing Encyclopedia* (So. Lake Tahoe, CA: Prudential Publishing, 1982), 360 (hereafter cited as *Quick Printing*); and Strauss, *Printing,* 347.

28.   Friday, *Quick Printing,* 360; and Brian S. Cook. Telephone Interview with the author, 6 April 1984. Cook is sales training instructor, Itek Graphic Systems, Rochester, NY (hereafter cited as Cook 4/6).

29.   Jack Klasnic, Inplant Printing Handbook, (Salem, NH: GAMA Communication, 1981), 134, 142–3 (hereafter cited as *Inplant*).

30.   Cook 4/6; and Friday, *Quick Printing,* 381–2.

31. Friday, *Quick Printing,* 360.

32. Porte Publishing Company. "Instructions and Information," in *Franklin Offset Catalog,* Section (Salt Lake City, UT: Porte Publishing, 1980), 1–4.

33. William Friday. Telephone interview with the author, 16 January 1984, (hereafter cited as Friday, 1/16).

34. Klasnic, *Inplant,* 5–6.

35. Harold C. Durbin, Terminology, Printing and Computers (Easton, PA: Durbin Associates, 1980) 55 (hereafter cited as Computers); and Graphic Arts Technical Foundation; *Techno-Econom-Forecast 9, Prepress Automation: Opportunities 1980–1984* (Pittsburgh, PA: Graphic Arts Technical Foundation, 1979) 195 (hereafter cited as *Forecast 9*).

36. Xerox Corporation. *1983 Fact Book,* (Stamford Corporation, 1983), 8–9 (hereafter cited as Xerox Fact).

37. Graphic Arts Technical Foundation. *Forecast 9,* 195; and Marcia A. DeMinco. Personal correspondence with author, 8 December 1983. DeMinco is coordinator, Public Information Center, Xerox Corporation, Stamford, CT (hereafter cited as DeMinco 12/8).

38. National Association of Printers and Lithographers, *New Developments in Reproduction Technology are Affecting Markets* (Teaneck, NJ: National Association of Printers and Lithographers, 1983), 1 (hereafter cited as *Developments in Reproduction).*

39. Howard K. Britt, "The Upheaval in Copying/Duplicating," *The New England Printer and Publisher,* (July 1978): after cited as "Upheaval."

40. Graphic Arts Technical Foundation. *Forecast 9,* 196.

41. U.S. Department of Commerce. *Quality Typesetting,* 87.

42. U.S. Department of Labor. Bureau of Labor Statistics. "Printing and Publishing," by Robert V. Critchlow in *The Impact of Technology on Labor in Five Industries,* bulletin 2137 (Washington, DC: GPO, 1982), 41 (hereafter cited as "Publishing").

43. Seybold, *Modern Photocomposition,* 39; and Strauss, *Printing,* 65–77.

44. Seybold, *Modern Photocomposition,* 39–43.

45. James E. Horne. Interview with the author, 24 August 1983 (hereafter cited as Horne, 8/24).

46. National Composition Association. Division of the Printing Industries of America, Inc. "Bench Mark Production Reports" (Arlington, VA: National Composition Association, March 1983) (hereafter cited as NCA).

47. Strauss, *Printing,* 181, 254.

48. Strauss, *Printing,* 259.

49. Fred C. Munson, *Labor Relations in the Lithographic Industry,* (Cambridge, MA: Harvard University Press, 38–39 (hereafter cited as *Labor Relations).*

50. Strauss, *Printing,* 260.

51. Strauss, *Printing,* 170; and Raymond J. Luca. Personal correspondence with the author, 14 March 1984. Luca is director of marketing, LogETronics, Inc., Springfield, VA (hereafter cited as Luca, 3/14); and U.S. Department of Labor. "Publishing," 17.

52. Strauss, *Printing,* 261–2; and U.S. Department of Labor, "Publishing," 17.

53. Cook 4/6.

54. Eastman-Kodak Company. Kodak Graphic Arts Industry Manpower Study (Rochester, NY: Eastman-Kodak Co. 1973), 219 (hereafter cited as *Manpower).*

55. Munson, *Labor Relations,* 40–1.

56. Strauss, *Printing,* 325.

57. Munson, *Labor Relations,* 41.

58. Strauss, *Printing,* 347.

59. Daniels 9/30, and Friday, *Quick Printing,* 361–2.

60. Simich 8/25.

61. Union Employers of America, "The Future," 9.

62. GATF. *Techno-Economic Forecast 10: Impact of New Technology on Graphic Arts Work Forces: 1980–1984*, (Pittsburgh, PA: GATF, 1980), 162–3 (hereafter cited as *Forecast 10*).

63. Daniels, 9/30.

64. Daniels, 12/8, and Joseph Scheldrick. Telephone Interview with the author, 15 September 1983.

3

Craft Decline
Measurement

INTRODUCTION

Quantification of the influence of technology on occupational skills is now necessary to test the craft decline hypothesis, which shall measure both the reduction in craft training and the decline in proportional skilled employment. The proportion of craft employment in printing is then estimated and its implications are analyzed.

The first measure of printing production skill decline is the historical change in the length of time needed for on-the-job training. Craft apprenticeship is the source of specialized printing skills and serves as a measure of craft production skills. The chapter reviews the years of training required in union and nonunion apprenticeship programs between 1948 and 1982. A composite printer's craft skill index is constructed by multiplying the years of nonunion apprenticeship by the comparable percentage of industry occupational employment. New processes are then related to the length of the compositors', preparation workers' and press craft workers' apprenticeships.

The relative increase in unskilled employment separately measures the reduced demand for craft production. The rising unskilled employment of substitute suppliers outside of the commercial printing industry indexes the reduction in craft production demand. This chapter begins by establishing the basis by which unskilled labor competes with printing craftsmen. To this end, historical production employment figures for private and quick printers who utilize these unskilled processes provide a measure for the substitution of unskilled for craft labor. An estimate of the printing industry labor market is then constructed on the basis of competition rather than the use of traditional letterpress and offset processes.

50

The craft decline hypothesis suggests a decline in the proportion of craft workers as a percent of total production employment. Proportional craft employment for commercial printers (SIC 275), the competitive labor market and the larger publishing and printing industry (SIC 27) is reviewed.

CRAFT TRAINING

Labor in the commercial printing industry can be divided into craft, semiskilled and unskilled categories. Craftworkers are divided into the four trades of typesetting, preparation, press, and bindery. The distinguishing characteristic of a printing craftworker is the ability to set up and independently operate all equipment within that craft jurisdiction. Semiskilled and unskilled industry workers require craftsmen to set up and supervise the operation of process equipment.

In terms of employment, the two dominant categories of semi-skilled industry workers require some industry specific training while unskilled labor requires none. For instance, in 1965 nonunion assistant pressmen required half the six year apprenticeship of a press craft worker. A press assistant loads and unloads paper, and assists the pressman in the overall operation of the press. Assistant bookbinders require two years of training, as opposed to the five years required of a bindery craftsman. The "bindery II," or assistant bookbinder, loads and unloads machines and performs handwork such as collating, labelling, and wrapping.[1]

Apprenticeship is the accepted way of entering skilled printing occupations. Craftworkers in the printing trades learn their jobs after they start work as an apprentice. Apprenticeship programs may be highly structured as in union and some nonunion shops. A vague arrangement is often found in the majority of nonunion plants.[2]

In general, the training of union craftsmen is probably superior to nonunion training. Simich states, ". . . unions have a larger, formal training program comprised of a logical sequence of presenting skills required for production. Formal union training is more productive than the inconsistent, informal training of the non-union shops."[3]

Union apprenticeship regulations in force from 1958 to 1983 require the apprentice to receive comprehensive, all-around training in a particular craft. Craftsmen who completed their apprenticeships in 1983 are required to perform the same range of functions as 1958 training program graduates. Regulating the type of work apprentices may perform serves to protect them from being frozen in some special job in which they have little opportunity to learn the general work of the trade. Apprenticeship programs also often include required reading, attendance at classes, school work, and examinations at regular intervals. Most comprehensive statements of apprenticeship curriculum specify on-the-job training classes and reviews. These are outlined in International Typographical Union (ITU) contracts. While the industry continually advocates the need for more theoretical training to keep up with the new technologies, as of 1983 on-the-job training was still the basis of apprenticeship and post-apprenticeship training.[4]

Apprentices are initially employed at a relatively low wage that is annually adjusted as their skills increase. Compositors in New York receive 30 percent of the journeyman's rate during the first year of apprenticeship and work up gradually until they receive 75 percent of the full pay during their sixth and last year as apprentices.

Entry into an apprenticeship is difficult due to the attitudes of both unions and employers. Unions restrict the number of apprentices in order to protect their membership against unemployment. Employers limit the number of apprentices because of the cost of training.[5]

During the 24-year period under study here (1958–82), the comprehensiveness and methods of training were consistent. Union contracts, in particular, indicate the complete range and consistency in training programs. Contracts between the Pressman and Bindery Unions and the League each include a statement similar to one found in the Typographical Union Contract: "It is the intent of the League and Union that apprentices will receive training in all phases of the trade...." Apprenticeship consistency is indicated by almost identical language defining courses of training in the League contracts with the Typographical Union between 1955 and 1975, the Pressman's Union between 1950 and 1979, and the Binder's Union between 1958 and 1978.[6]

Measurement of Craft Skill

One needs to look specifically at the changes in length of training resulting from the introduction of the new processes to determine the relation between technology and craft training. The influence of innovations in printing technology is measured here by the historical training requirements of New York City union and nonunion craftsmen. The decline in the number of years' training reflects the trend and not the measure of skill in any particular year. Industry-wide acceptance of the new training requirements is likely to occur over a short period—after the influence of new production processes is apparent.

Union training requirements are included in all collective bargaining agreements signed between the Printers' League Section of the Printing Industries of Metropolitan New York, Inc. and Typographical Local No. 6, Pressmen's Local No. 51 and GAIU Bindery Local No.

Table 3.1: Union Printing Industry Craftsman Apprenticeship Requirements, 1947–82, *(years' training required)*

Year	Typesetting (Hot)	Preparation	Press	Bindery
1947–49	6	6	6	5
1950–1970	6	4.5	4.5	5
1971–1982	4	4	4	5

Source: Compiled by the author.

119-B. Table 3.1, Apprenticeship Requirements, 1947–82, summarizes these data.

In an interview on April 7, 1984, James E. Horne, executive director of the Printing Industries of Metropolitan New York, advised the author that waivers are available for apprenticeship applicants who had prior experience as proof press operators in the composing room. The effect of these waivers was to occasionally reduce the hot type apprenticeship term from 6 to 4 years prior to 1971.

International Typographical Union Local No. 6 did not specify an apprenticeship training program for cold type in its contracts during the period 1958–78. As a practice designed to avoid layoffs, a journeyman who had completed his hot type apprenticeship program would retrain on a typewriter keyboard and acquire an understanding of any new cold type process skills on the job. In 1975, the Local No. 6 contract deleted the appprenticeship program because of cold type process introduction.

The decline in the terms of union apprenticeship in composition, preparation, and press reflect the relative skill reduction in three of the four stages of printing production. While the purpose of examining the historical training data is to measure relative skill, the length of union apprenticeships reflects both skill and bargaining power. Comparable nonunion training data is presented to offset the direct effect of bargaining power upon training requirements.

Nonunion training requirements were collected from "Recommended Standards of Wages and Hours" published by the Master Printers' Section of the Printing Industries of Metropolitan New York, Inc. Richard Anderson, executive vice-president of the association, states that approximately 30 members of the association's Labor Committee meet twice each year to determine what standards (including training) would be required for members. The Labor Committee represents a broad spectrum of opinions and includes in its consideration comparable union training programs. Table 3.2, Non-Union Printing Industry Craftsmen Apprenticeship Requirements (1950-1982) summarizes this data.[7]

Table 3.2:   **Nonunion Printing Industry Craftsmen Apprenticeship Require-ments, 1950–82,** *(years' training required)*

| Year | Typesetting | | Preparation | Press | Bindery |
	Hot	Cold			
1950–1952	6	NA	NA	6	4.5
1953–1958	6	NA	6	6	4
1959	6	2	6	6	4
1960–1966	6	2	6	6	5
1967–1968	6	1.5	6	6	5
1969	6	1.5	4	4	5
1970–1982	4	1	4	3	5

Source: Complied by the author.

Note: Master Printers' Section discontinued publication of apprenticeship requirements in 1982.

Within the Master Printers' occupational classifications, a hot type craftsman is defined to be a machine compositor. Prior to 1961, the length of apprenticeship was 5½ years for either a hand compositor or a proofreader. The corresponding term for a machine compositor was 6 years. All craft classifications were combined in 1961 and 6 years of apprenticeship were required. This modification was similar to that found in the union training programs themselves.

Cold typesetting training requirements are based upon the expert industry opinion of James E. Horne, given during interviews on 28 June and 16 July 1982.

Within the same classification, craft pressmen are defined to be "cylinder" pressmen prior to 1953 and "offset" pressmen between 1953 and 1962. These two categories were combined in 1963. Prior to 1963, the nonunion printers specified a four-year term of apprenticeship for a less skilled "platen" pressman. The length of union apprenticeship for "platen," "cylinder," and "offset" pressmen is identical in the *Standards of Apprenticeship for Pressmen* published by the Joint Negotiating Committee of the Printers' League Section, New York Employing Printers Association, Inc., and New York Printing Pressmen's Union, Local No. 51, May 24, 1950 as amended December 24, 1951 and April 1, 1953 respectively.

No distinction is made between "cylinder" and "offset" pressmen in the Local 51 revised rules governing apprentices published in the "Book and Job Office Contract" for 1971–74 between the Printers' League Section and the New York Printing Pressmen and Offset Workers Union Local No. 51.

The length of apprenticeship, except for the amount of time needed to learn photocomposition, varies to a consistently small degree between union and nonunion training programs. Nonunion compositors trained for the same six-year term until 1971, when a four-year apprenticeship program for hot type process became uniform in both union and nonunion plants. Union apprenticeship programs were still designed for the displaced hot type methods as late as 1974, despite the widespread use of new photocomposition processes. Nonunion preparation and press operators trained a uniform 1.5 years more than their union counterparts until 1970. Beginning in 1971, nonunion and union preparation training was identical in length, while union pressmen trained one year less than their nonunion counterparts. The fact that union followed nonunion declines in apprenticeship training length suggests that the sudden recognition in 1971 was indeed due to acceptance of the skill decline that had occurred prior to 1971. What small historical difference exists in the lengths of union and nonunion training programs reflects the judgment of two separate training committees.[8]

James Horne, executive vice-president, Printing League Section, Printing Industries of Metropolitan New York, Inc., was the employer-representative who negotiated the reduction in apprenticeship requirements summarized in Table 3.1. Horne establishes the institutional mediation between technological change and craft training; he states that the shortened length of union craft worker training, while caused by new and simplified processes, is only put into effect after collective bargaining. In addition, he reports the sequence of events which led to the reduction in training in 1970 indicated in Table 3.1. The decline in union apprenticeship began with the decision made at the national convention of the ITU to reduce the period of typesetting apprenticeship from six to four years. In 1971, Local No. 6 of the ITU proposed a shorter term of apprenticeship. This was accepted by employers, which in turn triggered Local No. 51 of the Pressmen's Union also to review and ultimately reduce the length of preparation and press craftworker apprenticeship.[9]

Jack Simich, education director of the GATF, concurs that the training requirements summarized in Table 3.2 are appropriate for each stage of production as well as for the national printing industry as a whole. Molloy and Horne also confirm that the New York training requirements are representative of the national printing industry.[10]

CRAFT SKILL INDEX

This study's craft skill index measures the variation in skill, over time, within five stages of printing production. As stated earlier, a composite printer's craft skill index is constructed by multiplying the years of nonunion apprenticeship by the comparable percentage of industry occupational employment. The length of nonunion training shown in Table 3.2 measures the redefinition or variation in the level of craftsman skill. Occupational employment data presented in Table 3.3 weigh the relative effect of new technology on each of the five printing crafts.

Occupational Employment Estimates

Statistics on employment by occupation in the commercial printing industry (SIC 275) were collected from employers by the Bureau of Labor Statistics during 1970, 1977, and 1980. Annual labor hours for craft occupational employment statistics are drawn from a sample of establishments listed in the unemployment insurance lists. It is a systematic probability sample of establishments stratified by industry and employment size class. The initial stage of data collection involved largely mail collection but also included some personal visits to certain large establishments.[11]

Between survey years, a linear interpolation of occupational ratios is based upon the proximity to the prior or future Bureau of Labor Statistics surveys in 1970, 1977, and 1980. The estimating formula used in Table 3.3 is:

$$R_t = S_p (1 - W_p) + S_f W_p$$

Where:

R_t = Annual estimate of occupational employment

S_p = Prior annual occupational employment ratio published by the Bureau of Labor Statistics

S_f = Future occupational employment ratio published by the Bureau of Labor Statistics.

W_p = Weight of the intervening years between prior (Y_p) and future (Y_f) Bureau of Labor Statistics Employment ratio.

$$W_p = \frac{Y_x - Y_p}{Y_f - Y_p}$$

Example:

The estimate for 1971 of hot type craft compositor employment is based upon prior 1970 and relatively future 1977 occupational employment ratios.

$$R_t = S_p (1 - W_p) + S_f W_p$$
$$R_t = .253 (1 - .1428) + .134 (.1428)$$
$$R_t = .2167 + (.0191)$$
$$R_t = .236$$

Table 3.3: Craft Occupational Employment—Commercial Printing Industry, SIC 275, 1970–80, *(percent of total industry craft employment)*

Year	Data Source	Typesetting Hot	Cold	Hot & Cold	Preparation	Press	Bindery
1970	Survey	.253	.025	.279	.191	.451	.078
1971	Estimate	.236	.026	.262	.200	.460	.078
1972	Estimate	.216	.027	.243	.206	.472	.078
1973	Estimate	.203	.027	.230	.216	.480	.077
1974	Estimate	.183	.028	.211	.225	.489	.074
1975	Estimate	.166	.028	.194	.234	.497	.074
1976	Estimate	.150	.028	.178	.240	.508	.074
1977	Survey	.134	.029	.163	.254	.516	.073
1978	Estimate	.124	.030	.154	.254	.527	.070
1979	Estimate	.118	.031	.149	.257	.534	.067
1980	Survey	.109	.032	.141	.257	.543	.064

Source: Compiled by the author.

Note: Comparable occupational employment data is unavailable after 1980 due to occupational reclassification.

Table 3.3 summarizes this craft occupational employment. These data weigh the relative effect of new technology within printing functions. Within each stage of production, the printers' craft skill index is calculated by multiplying the years of nonunion training by the comparable percent of industry occupational employment. The estimating formula for each craft index value is:

$$C_t = T_t E_t$$

Where:

C_t = Annual estimate of relative occupational skill within commercial printing industry (SIC 275).

T_t = Number of years training required in each printing craft occcupation.

E_t = Craft occupational employment expressed as percent of total SIC 275 industry employment.

Example:
The hot typesetting craft index value for 1980 is calculated as follows:

$$C_t = (4) (.109)$$
$$C_t = .436$$

Table 3.4: Printing Craft Skill Index, 1966–80

| Year | Typesetting | | Preparation | Press | Bindery | Sum of |
	Hot	Cold				Index Value
1966	1.518	.050	1.146	2.706	.390	5.81
1967	1.518	.038	1.146	2.706	.390	5.80
1968	1.518	.038	1.146	2.706	.390	5.80
1969	1.518	.038	.764	1.804	.390	4.51
1970	1.012	.025	.764	1.353	.390	3.54
1971	.944	.026	.800	1.380	.390	3.54
1972	.864	.027	.824	1.416	.390	3.52
1973	.812	.027	.864	1.440	.385	3.53
1974	.732	.028	.900	1.440	.370	3.47
1975	.664	.028	.936	1.491	.370	3.49
1976	.600	.028	.960	1.524	.370	3.48
1977	.536	.029	1.016	1.548	.365	3.49
1978	.496	.030	1.016	1.581	.350	3.47
1979	.472	.031	1.028	1.602	.335	3.47
1980	.436	.032	1.028	1.629	.320	3.45

Source: Compiled by the author.

Note: Since three digit occupational employment data are not available prior to 1970, this table assumes that industry occupational ratios remained constant between 1966 and 1970.

Table 3.4 summarizes the printing craft skill index values between 1966 and 1980. Since three digit occupational employment data are not available prior to 1970, Table 3.4 assumes that industry occupational ratios are constant between 1966 and 1970.

Skill Index Interpretation

The Printing Craft Skill Index of Table 3.4 measures the composite decline in industry craft skills that accompanied the introduction of new technology. The sum of Index values declined by almost half, from 5.81 in 1966 to 3.45 in 1980.

Composition craftsmen training requirements declined from six years in 1958 to one year in 1978 as photocomposition processes displaced hot typesetting. What required six years of training for hot type operators to master, first- and second-generation photocomposition devices required only two years. Following the introduction of third generation CRT photocomposition systems in 1967, training continued to decline until it reached only one year in 1970.

The decline of two years in preparation and three years in press training since 1958 reflects the continuous mechanization of hand operations with the application of electronic controls to printing equipment. In the late 1960s the widespread use of automated camera exposure and film processing devices caused the decline in training time for combination preparation craftsmen. By 1969, training time had declined from six to four years.

The impact of new technology upon the printers' skill index varies directly with the mechanization of hand operations and the degree of automatic control incorporated in production equipment. The cold type skill index values reflect the fact that all previously skilled typesetting functions except make-up and proofreading were reduced to the unskilled level by the major innovation of CRT photocomposition. The skill index also registers the continuous erosion of craft preparation and press skills by minor innovations in those crafts.

COLOR PRINTING INCREASES CRAFT EMPLOYMENT

Proportional employment data obscures important trends in the continuing craft displacement by new production technologies. While craft decline may reduce the demand for skilled printers, an increase in the demand for craft-intensive full-color printing will also increase the demand for preparation and press workers. Full-color printing still requires preparation and press craftsmen for the traditional four-color lithographic process. The composition and bindery workers in the two bracketing stages of production are unaffected by an increase in the demand for color printing.

The major cause for the increased demand for full-color printing is the reduction in the unit cost that occurred between 1967 and 1984. The four-color process offers the advantages of the highest quality and the lowest unit cost of full-color reproduction.[12]

Table 3.5 indicates that the unit cost for full-color printed matter relative to nonfull-color work has declined by nearly half between 1965 and 1984. Since the typical number of units produced in each commercial printing industry order is under 10,000,[13] this table summarizes unit cost data on production runs of 1,000, 5,000, and 10,000 units.

This is, however, no clear measure of the growth in fullcolor printing after 1958. On the basis of a 1978 survey of commercial printers, the GATF indicates that an increase in the use of color in all segments of commercial printing except legal and financial is readily apparent. In order to index the growth in color printing, the GAFT utilizes the historical trend of four-color advertising in consumer magazines. Table 3.6 indicates that the proportion of full-color printing increased signifi-

Table 3.5   Ratio of Four-Color Process Unit Cost to Single-Color Printing
            Unit Cost, 1965–84 *(page rate)*

| Year | Unit Quantity | | |
	1,000	5,000	10,000
1965	17.14	13.99	12.01
1966	17.08	13.88	11.87
1967	NA	NA	NA
1968	16.85	13.72	11.79
1969	16.74	13.65	11.74
1970	16.64	13.47	11.51
1971	9.83	8.69	8.01
1972	9.63	8.55	7.91
1973	9.89	8.70	8.00
1974	9.90	8.71	8.00
1975	9.89	8.71	8.00
1976	9.96	8.75	8.05
1977	9.12	8.19	7.64
1978	9.09	8.17	7.63
1979	8.99	8.11	7.60
1980	8.41	7.70	7.29
1981	8.23	7.59	7.20
1982	8.07	7.45	7.10
1983	8.18	7.49	7.10
1984	8.48	7.65	7.19

Source: Compiled by the author.
Notes:
   1.   Unit cost of four color process $8\frac{1}{2}$ x 11″ page (without bleed) printed one side in yellow, magenta, cyan and black from camera ready flexible art is the sum of negative, flat, plate and press work costs. The cost of paper is excluded.
   2.   In 1971, the unit rate for a set of four color process negatives declined by approximately 50 percent from $230.10 in 1970 to $116.62 in 1971. The dramatic decline in the cost of process negatives is due to the conversion from hand methods to automated color scanners as noted on page 8, "Section D Copy, Negatives, Plates, Press Work," *Franklin Offset Catalog,* 1970 and 1971.
   3.   In 1977, progressive press proofs were deleted at the unit cost of $58.00. In order to make the data comparable, $58.00 was added to the unit cost of process color printing in 1977 and thereafter.

cantly between 1966 and 1978. The GATF confirmed this increasing trend in color printing during interviews with a "large number of industry artists, accounting executives, magazine sales executives and printers."[14]

A more aggregate index of the historical production of full-color printing is also available from the GATF. Table 3.7 indicates that while a unit estimate of nonfull-color production increased from 100 to 140.4 between 1967 and 1984, full-color output more than doubled. The

Table 3.6: Trends in One-, Two-, and Four-Color Advertising Printing *(percent of magazine advertisements)*

| Year | Distribution of Printing | | |
	Four-Color	Two-Color	One-Color
1966	39.7	8.0	52.3
1967	42.2	7.6	50.2
1968	43.3	6.5	50.2
1969	44.5	6.2	49.3
1970	43.9	5.9	50.2
1971	46.6	5.1	48.3
1972	47.9	4.8	47.3
1973	49.2	5.1	45.7
1974	49.8	5.4	44.8
1975	50.0	5.0	45.0
1976	52.2	4.6	43.2
1977	54.8	4.3	40.9
1978	57.7	3.8	38.5

Source: Graphic Arts Technical Foundation (GATF) TechnoEconomic Forecast 8: The Future of Color Printing, 1979-1983, (Pittsburgh, PA: GATF, 1979), 57.

Table 3.7: Commercial Printing Industry Production Index of Full-Color Printing, 1967–84 (1967 = 100)

Year	Total Commercial Printing	Full-Color Printing	Other Printing
1967	100.0	100.0	100.0
1968	104.1	100.6	106.3
1969	109.7	106.7	111.7
1970	108.7	104.1	111.9
1971	107.8	104.6	111.0
1972	115.2	118.9	112.4
1973	122.8	125.8	120.5
1974	123.7	124.3	123.2
1975	118.4	107.3	119.5
1976	130.2	133.9	127.2
1977	136.8	149.5	125.6
1978	141.1	163.5	120.2
1979	148.2	171.8	124.6
1980	152.2	175.2	129.7
1981	159.1	180.1	138.4
1982	160.0	181.9	137.5
1983	169.9	204.6	132.0
1984	191.4	233.1	140.4

Source: Michael G. Coulson, Senior Market Analyst, Graphic Arts Technical Foundation, letter of May 24, 1985.

Note: The above table is based upon Federal Reserve Board (FRB) industrial output data for printing and publishing (SIC 27). FRB data has been adjusted to exclude newspapers, and include full-color share of newspaper inserts, direct mail, magazines, catalogs as well as coated paper shipments.

significant increase in the output of craft-intensive full-color printing compensates for the partial and full displacement of craft skills within the printing industry between 1967 and 1984.

LABOR MARKET COMPETITION

While the printers' skill index supports the craft decline hypothesis, it is necessary to use a different method to quantify the increased rate of substitution of unskilled labor for craft production techniques because the printers' skill index does not consider new processes that require only unskilled labor. In order to measure the displacement of craftworkers, this section will identify the relative skills, as well as the location of competition in a labor market segmented between craft and noncraft labor. In the production of noncraft products, in-plant and quick printers substitute for commercial printing industry craftworkers. In order to measure the decline in craft employment, this section will subsequently estimate the historical production employment of substitute suppliers utilizing new, unskilled processes.

In-plant printers, by definition, carry out printing in a firm primarily engaged in some business other than printing or publishing. Ordinarily, they perform work for the exclusive use of the firm itself. Generally, none of this work is sold commercially. This type of printing usually occurs in larger companies with operations that require a considerable amount of printed materials. Also known as captive printing, it utilizes a photocopying device in a separate department or even in a completely segregated plant.[15]

Expert opinion indicates that private plants offer three advantages to their owner: convenience, lower cost, and security. The location of private plants on customer sites is an obvious source of convenience. Though in-plant plants may have lower costs, data concerning the relative costs of commercial and in-plant printers are not available in sufficient quantity to make a clear determination possible. The third advantage of in-plant plants is the security of not having sensitive information leave the company's premises. Michael Bruno cites the in-house production of all materials relating to the Eastman-Kodak Instant Camera as an example of this. He credits it for the surprise introduction of that camera.[16]

The second of the two substitute suppliers, quick printers, are vigorously penetrating the commercial printing market with convenience or while-you-wait service. The National Association of Quick Printers (NAQP) defines quick printing as:

... that segment of commercial printing which is characterized by equipment, specifically duplicating equipment with less than 187 square inches of printing surface with no more than two form rollers, and facilities capable of providing while-you-wait service with camera ready originals most frequently in short runs (under 1,000 impressions), generally by line copy reproduced in black ink and operated at retail basis.[17]

Relative Skill Levels of Commercial, In-plant, and Quick Printers

It is possible to establish the relative skill levels of commercial, in-plant, and quick printers by determining the type of process, the location of the equipment that requires the lower levels of skill, and the complexity of printed matter of each supplier. Chapters 2 and 3 establish the level of skill employed in commercial plants utilizing lithography. The U. S. Department of Commerce classifies commercial printers as those who sell to the public, employ lithography, and produce the complete range of printed materials. The six major categories of printed products in commercial printing are: magazines and periodicals, labels and wrappers, catalogs and directories, financial and legal, advertising, and other. Only book printing (SIC 2732) and manifold business forms (SIC 2761) are not included in commercial printing (SIC 275).[18]

The choice of production equipment determines the level of operator skill. The skill level of traditional offset lithography thus established, this section will now identify the skill requirements of operators in new photo-direct offset and electrostatic processes. Manufacturers of photo-direct offset and electrostatic equipment specify that unskilled labor can operate their equipment. The major manufacturer of photo-direct press equipment, for instance, states that the training required to operate that equipment declined from three days in 1955 to one day in 1978. Photo-direct platemaking equipment requires less than one day of training according to its manufacturer, Itek. A representative of Xerox indicates that operator training on that firm's largest equipment decreased from 16 hours in 1974 to 10 hours in 1983.[19]

In-plant printers utilize photo-direct offset and electrostatic processes less often than commercial printing plants and quick printers. The A. B. Dick Company estimates that 45 percent of the unit sales of its presses is to in-plant printers, while another 27 percent is to quick printers. Only 28 percent of its photo-direct sales is to commercial printers. During the 1970s, quick printers purchased 60 percent of the photo-direct platemakers sold by Itek. Estimates for 1980 indicate that 30,000 large electrostatic duplicators manufactured by Eastman-Kodak and Xerox were installed in the United States. An earlier study indicates that only 4 percent of the 1,033 commercial printers responding to the survey utilized electrostatic processes.[20]

While in-plant printing existed prior to World War II, its prevalence increased dramatically after the introduction of the new photocomposition, photo-direct offset, and electrostatic processes. The founding of the In-Plant Management Association in 1963 is indicative of the recent growth of private printers. Robert Baker, association president, estimates that in-plant sales increased ten-fold between 1958 and 1982. It is the conclusion of the Battelle study (cited earlier) that new printing technologies "oriented towards short-runs, rapid turnaround and reduced operation skills have resulted in lower cost reproduction techniques and have greatly accelerated the in-plant phenomenon."[21]

Specifically, there was a rapid expansion of in-plant printing following the introduction of the Xerox 914 in 1959 and the Xerox 9200 in 1975. Because it is able to produce up to ten copies faster and more cheaply than a small press and without the mess of carbon paper, the Xerox 914 is seen by Bruno as the major impetus to in-plant, short-run printing. Likewise, Baker suggests that the introduction of the Xerox 9200 in 1974 enabled the in-plant plant to produce high-volume, single-color work more efficiently.[22]

The in-plant shop also uses equipment with conventional graphic arts capabilities in the prepress, press, and finishing areas. Only high-speed photocopiers are generally included as printing equipment. Surveys conducted by the In-Plant Management Association indicate that well over 90 percent of in-plant printers use offset printing equipment and 50 percent use electrostatic printing equipment. In addition, surveys conducted by A. F. Lewis indicate that 40 percent of these plants have phototypesetting equipment, 90 percent pre-press, and 80 percent bindery and other finishing equipment.[23]

Market Segmentation: Craft and Noncraft Labor

In order to locate the two sources of substitution for union craftworkers, this section defines the segmentation which exists in the labor market. No single market for commercial printing exists. This industry produces products ranging from textbooks to colorful magazines, neither of which require the same degree of operator skill, nor are they usually made by the same firm. The labor market is segmented in two dimensions—by the type of product sold, and by the geographic extent of the market. Whenever the boundaries for each of these two market dimensions are well-defined as, for example, when buyers of color printing will not accept advertising material printed only in black

Diagram 3.1. Labor Market Segmentation

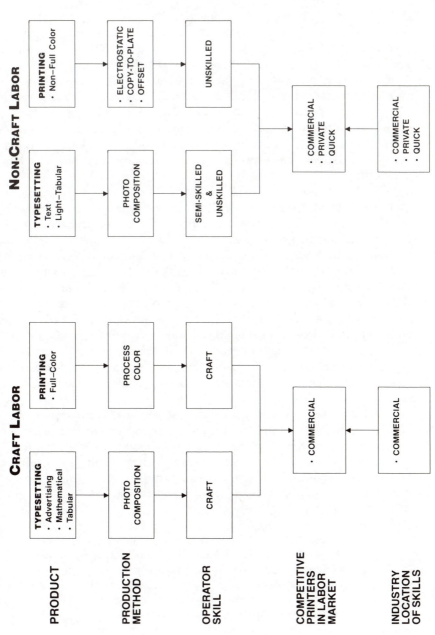

65

ink, then the market for color printing is said to be "insulated." The degree of insulation in each of these two market dimensions varies over the range of commercially printed products. Competition within the product market is the subject of this present section, while the geographic dimensions of the market appear in a later chapter.[24]

The type of product and the location of workers possessing the relevant skills determines labor market competition. The physical characteristics of any printed product sequentially determine the production method and, by so doing, determine the skill of the work force producing that product. And labor market competition occurs among those firms that require that level of skill. Diagram 3.1 illustrates the interrelation of printed product characteristics and the location of skills. In order to specify labor market competition, this section identifies craft and noncraft products, establishes location of craft skills, and defines the respective markets for craft and noncraft labor competition.

Printed products can be divided into those that require traditional craft methods and those that do not. In the typesetting labor market sector, the most difficult work requires craft workers and includes the composition of advertisements as well as mathematical and tabular matter.[25] In the case of advertising copy, it is the wide range and mixing of type styles and sizes that makes the task so difficult. Similarly, mathematical and tabular matter of more than three columns creates difficulty in character alignment. Noncraft typesetting comprises all other matter not classified within the above three categories of complex work. Noncraft products make up the bulk of typesetting and are generally categorized as straight matter and light tabular matter made up in a standard format. Books, magazines, newsletters, and telephone directories are examples of copy that can be set by semiskilled and unskilled labor.

In the printing, or nontypesetting, sector of the industry, the use of craft and noncraft methods hinges on the use of full color. The distinction between full-color and nonfull-color work is important because it identifies that craft sector of the market where commercial printers have been insulated from competition. Within the printing sector are preparation, press, and bindery workers. Strauss defines full-color printing as follows:

> Full color printing is used for the reproduction of original images which contain an unrestricted play of colors. Examples of such colorful original images are fine-art paintings, color photographs and commercial artwork made without restrictions as to the number of colors. These original images cannot be produced in any other way than by full color printing.[26]

Multicolor printing, or printing in several color inks, differs in one deci-
sive point from full-color printing. In multicolor printing the final product shows a limited number of colors, whereas in full-color printing the
finished product presents a wide gamut of colors comprising a large
portion of the color spectrum.

The four-color process has the advantage of producing the highest
quality of full-color reproduction at the lowest unit cost. Instead of indi-
vidually matching each color of the original artwork with a specific color
ink, the printer reproduces the whole color spectrum using only three
different colors of ink, each of which are apparently completely
unrelated to any individual color in the original image. Without the
four-color technique, one would need a separate image carrier and press
run for every different color. Twenty-five, 50 and even more would be
required for a reproduction that in full-color printing is done in four
different printings, with four different printing carriers, and using four
different printing inks of the correct colors.[27]

It is possible to produce full-color printing only through a craft
method. In lithography, this is commonly referred to as the four-color
process. Munson, Strauss, industry experts Coulson and Simich, as well
as trade literature all separately indicate the need for craft skills in the
reproduction of full-color work. The four-color techniques used in the
reproduction of full-color still require skilled workers in preparation
and press functions in order to achieve the precise register of the four
colors superimposed upon one another. Technological change, then, creates segmentation in the product market between full-color and nonfull-
color printed matter, the distinction hinging upon the number of
halftones used. A halftone is the reproduction of continuous tone
artwork, such as a photograph, through a grid pattern or contact screen,
which converts the image into dots of various sizes.[28]

With full color, a series of two or more halftone plates produces
intermediate colors and shades. In theory, any full-color copy is reproducible from a combination of three primary colors (yellow, magenta,
cyan) and black. Neither electrophotography nor photo-direct offset
processes are capable of converting the original image into a large
enough number of dots of various sizes to produce the full color spectrum. Industry experts Lamparte and Scharfert agree that despite the
introduction of the Xerox 5600 Color Copier in 1974, the imaging characteristics of electrophotography in 1983 were still limited to the reproduction of line copy, text material, and, relative to lithography, coarse
continuous-tone pictures.[29]

In addition to the location of craft skills which will be examined
later, color printing remains in the commercial sector of the industry
because of economies of scale. The scale of multicolor equipment
exceeds the sum of the individual costs of an identical number of single-

color presses. That is, the cost of a four-color printing press will be in excess of four times the cost of similar one-color equipment.[30] Non-full-color printing, in contrast, requires no more than one halftone plate and is usually suitable for reproduction without using a halftone screen at all. The bulk of printed matter, indeed all printed matter, with the exception of full-color printing, is reproducible without craft methods by the unskilled operation of electrophotography and copy-to-plate methods.

Trade literature recognizes the possibilities in substituting photo-direct offset, or copy-to-plate, and electrostatic printing in the production of non-full-color work. The GATF states that copy-to-plate systems continue to replace conventional, commercial offset plates because there is currently no method for exposing metal plates directly to copy. A trade article published in 1977 estimates that there were 250,000 offset duplicators in use in the United States at that time. Additionally, Friday and Klasnic recognize the ability to substitute photo-direct offset methods in the printing of up to a few hundred copies of line work.[31]

Industry experts also recognize electrostatic printing as a process competitive with both photo-direct and conventional offset. According to Britt, electrostatic printing is less costly when producing under 100 copies of single-color alphanumeric and line copy on $8\frac{1}{2}$ x 11″ sheets. Both Friday and Klasnic discuss the substitution possibilities between electrostatic, photodirect offset, and conventional offset methods depending upon copy quality and quantity. In addition, they indicate the increasing competition being given to both photo-direct and conventional offset printing by electrostatic methods.[32]

After an exhaustive study of in-plant printing, GATF characterized the type of this output. The GATF listed in order of importance the following products: (1) forms; (2) catalogs, specifications, and price-/parts lists; (3) manuals; (4) newsletters and magazines; (5) reports; and (6) directories. Much of the printing done in-plant is short run and single color.[33]

In terms of products, what differentiate the commercial plant from the in-house plant are their requirements for craft production skills. Many people choose to produce the simpler jobs in-house and purchase the more complex jobs from commercial printers. The commercial printer bases his or her quality upon the skill and expertise needed to produce the more complex job. Industry sectors outside of commercial printing rarely produce full-color work. Commonly, in-house plants purchase color printing requiring the highest level of journeyman skills. These skills go beyond the capabilities of most in-house plants. In a separate study of color printing demand, the GATF concludes that very few in-plant employees are involved in color printing.[34]

According to Robert L. Schweiger, publisher of *Quick Printing Magazine* and a former president of NAQP, technological skill reduction is the cause for the growth in the quick printing industry. In discussing the penetration of quick printers into the commercial market, Schweiger states,

> Recent production announcements of leading industry manufacturers represent merely the next stage in the evolution of quick printing. The industry itself grew from technology which allowed relatively unskilled labor to perform printing tasks which previously could only be performed by skilled craftsmen. The recent introduction of automated duplicators, improved plate material, and innovations such as laser and ink-jet printing will further increase the impact of quick printers on the graphic arts.[35]

In a recent article, Piercy states that the most significant difference between quick and commercial printers is the type of product demand. Commercial printers of similar size tend to develop their markets in process color, whereas quick printers market the short-run, 8½ x 11″ format printing of one and two colors.[36]

The relative complexity of commercial printing production has been established by the GATF on the basis of surveys. Substitute suppliers, such as in-plant printers, tend to produce short-run, single-color work. Commercial printers, in turn, generally produce larger runs, color, and, as a rule, more complex work. The GATF concludes that the expertise of skilled, trained personnel available at a commercial printer is the characteristic that distinguishes them from in-plant printers.[37]

While seldom used by commercial printers, these conventional printing processes provide the primary basis of in-house and quick printing plant production. The standard equipment of in-house and quick printers that are competitive with commercial printers incorporates two of the major skill reducing innovations identified in Chapter 1: photo-direct offset and electrostatic equipment, and occasionally photocomposition devices.

In-plant and quick printers are the major competition for commercial printers. In 1942, for example, a U.S. Department of Labor study concluded that "private offers a major source of competition to the general commercial printer. . . . " Donald Piercy, in addition, states in an interview that in terms of market, the "quick printer is indistinguishable from the commercial printer." In its analysis of quick printing growth, Battelle concludes that quick printers have grown at the expense of commercial plants, predicting that with the increasing capabilities of electrostatic printing, traditional markets will be invaded even further.[38]

The Kodak study suggests that the reason for the commercial printing industry loss of its market to substitute suppliers is the lack of technological innovations in their printing processes. Kodak cites "Xerography" as the best example of how conventional printing has failed to serve the needs of the new product market. The electrostatic process has replaced the traditional communication and storage of office and other information through cumbersome, messy carbon paper. The photo-direct process also attempts to satisfy this information storage need.[39]

Technological change increases the overlap between commercial printers and substitute suppliers in the production of nonprocess printing. Since photo-direct offset and electrostatic processes require only unskilled operators and are primarily employed by private and quick printers, employment growth of private and quick printers provides a measure of substitution of unskilled for skilled printing production workers.

Commercial Printing Employment

The traditional commercial printing industry group (SIC 275) is defined by the Bureau of Labor Statistics in terms of product. The designation of commercial or job printing is a residual and contains the six major SIC product subdivisions of magazines, periodicals, labels and wrappers, catalogs and directories, financial and legal, advertising and screen printing. A seventh category, "other general job printing or nonclassified print," comprised 28 percent of commercial printing in 1977. Private and quick printing employment is not included within commercial printing employment data. The subject of this study, SIC 275, is the largest segment of the national printing industry in terms of value added, employment, and number of establishments.[40]

The printing industry labor market should be defined in terms of competition rather than subdivided by the traditional use of letterpress or offset processes. Union labor now competes with predominantly unskilled in-plant and quick printers. Historically, the supply of labor was restricted by the length of training and the specificity of skill required by antiquated production equipment. The three innovations of CRT photocomposition, photo-direct offset, and electrostatic printing have reduced the barriers to competition and increased the supply of labor competitive with union printers. This section of labor market estimates includes commercial, in-plant, and quick printing production employment.

Since commercial printing employment increased in the years between 1959 and 1980, inadequate attention has been paid to the growing competition of substitute suppliers. Table 3.8 indicates that commercial industry production employment alone increased by 140,000, or 71 percent. This is in contrast to an 84 percent total United States manufacturing production employment increase. Total printing employment increased 67 percent as opposed to general manufacturing employment increase of 79 percent.[41]

In-plant and Quick Printing Employment Estimate

In-plant and quick printing employment data, published in trade literature, are based upon estimates of the size distribution of such

Table 3.8 Commercial Printing Industry Employment, SIC 275, 1958–83 *(in thousands)*

Year	All Employees	Production Workers
1958	278.1	220.3
1959	284.0	225.0
1960	290.7	230.6
1961	292.4	232.2
1962	295.7	233.2
1963	296.7	232.6
1964	302.4	236.3
1965	309.3	241.9
1966	321.3	252.1
1967	331.4	259.5
1968	340.1	265.7
1969	350.4	272.6
1970	354.2	274.6
1971	345.6	268.6
1972	354.2	272.5
1973	359.2	276.0
1974	358.9	274.3
1975	347.5	261.7
1976	352.2	262.1
1977	367.8	272.1
1978	390.5	288.7
1979	407.1	302.5
1980	413.7	307.3
1981	419.7	308.8
1982	425.7	312.1
1983	436.7	318.9

Source: U. S. Department of Labor. Bureau of Labor Statistics. *Employment and Earnings in the United States, 1909–1978,* bulletin 1312–11 supplement to *Employment and Earnings,* revised establishment data (Washington, DC: GPO, 1984).

plants and on their probable total number. Unfortunately, the Department of Commerce does not have a separate industrial classification for either in-plant or quick printers. In an interview, Charles R. Cook advised that an insignificant number of in-plant and quick printers are included in SIC 275 commercial printing census data. Technically, all in-plant printers are excluded from the Census of Manufacturers' data by definition. In-plant data are only included as commercial printing if production at one site is for use at one or more locations of the same company. Cook knew of only two cases where large in-plant facilities received the consent of the reporting company to maintain separate books and records for the printing plant. Such consent would enable them to be included in the *Census* data. In addition, he estimated that less than 10 percent of the quick printers were included as commercial printers in census reports.[42]

Measurement of in-plant employment is difficult because it is not distinguishable from the operation of its owner. Consequently, private printing is not reported as a separate entity to any U. S. Government Agency. However, in order to exclude small office copiers, recent surveys have agreed on the following definition of in-plant printing:

> Printing activities within a firm classified under something other than printing or publishing, using at least one item of recognized graphic arts equipment requiring at least one full-time operator, and producing output for the exclusive use of the firm owning the printing facility.[43]

However, an estimate of the in-plant employment increase can be made on the basis of both published data and expert opinion. A recent study, *In-Plant Printing,* estimates the number of plants in 1967, 1975, and 1983. In addition, the in-house plant study estimates the total 1983 employment to be 651,880 with 8.6 employees per shop. If we assume the average plant employment remained constant between 1967 and 1983, then total employment of the in-plant printing industry can be estimated between 1967 and 1983.[44]

Holding the average plant employment constant implies that industry employment will vary at a rate equal to the increase in the number of plants. Thus, the three-fold increase in the number of in-house plants from 25,000 in 1967 to 75,800 in 1983 implies an equal increase in in-house printing plant employment during the same period. Two authors of previous in-plant industry studies corroborate the three-fold increase in private plant employment between 1967 and 1983. Table 3.9 estimates the increase of private plant employment since 1967.[45]

A third estimate, and the basis of quick printing employment data presented in Table 3.10, is an extrapolation of "Franchised Printing and

Table 3.9:   In-plant Employment Estimate 1967–83 *(production workers)*

Industry	1967	1970	1975	1980	1983
In-Plant Printing	161,250	265,160	438,600	469,883	506,325

Source: Compiled by the author.
Notes:
1. Annual employment estimates are calculated by multiplying the number of plants by average plant employment. Average in-plant printing employment is assumed to be constant between 1967 and 1983. In-plant employment is also assumed to increase equally in the years between 1967, 1975, and 1983.
2. In order to be comparable with commercial printing industry production employment data, total in-plant employment is reduced by 25 percent. Production employment is assumed to be 75 percent of total in-plant printing industry employment.

Copying Services" data published by the Department of Commerce, Bureau of Industrial Economics. Expert opinion indicates that the total number of industry establishments are estimated by multiplying the reported number of franchise printers by 3.5.[46] Multiplying the ratio of 3.5 to each of 4,352 franchises yields 15,232 quick printing plants employing 45,696 in 1983. While expert opinion indicates that the industry began in 1967,[47] U. S. Department of Commerce data are available only since 1969. Quick printing employment is estimated to be zero in 1958.

Due to the continuous erosion of craft production demand, the labor market competitive with union printers is estimated by combining the production of the commercial printing industry with estimates of in-plant and quick plant employment. Despite the absolute growth in employment, commercial printing production employment declined in relation to in-plant and quick printing. Between 1970 and 1983 commercial printing production workers declined from 51 percent to 37 percent of the labor market. Table 3.10 estimates the labor market competitive with union printers.

Table 3.10: Union Printers Competitive Labor Market Estimate, Selected Years 1958-1985 *(production workers)*

Industry	1958	1970	1980	1983	Employment Increase (1970–83)
Commercial	220,300	274,600	307,300	319,900	16%
In-plant	NA	265,160	469,883	506,325	91%
Quick	-0-	2,590	24,494	34,272	____
Total Labor	NA	542,350	801,677	860,497	59%

Source: Compiled by the author.

PROPORTIONAL CRAFT EMPLOYMENT

The craft decline hypothesis suggests that craft workers, as a percent of total industry employment, should decline after the introduction of new production processes. Proportional craft employment data are estimated in printing and publishing (SIC 27), commercial printing (SIC 275), and the combined labor market of commercial, in-plant, and quick printers. As anticipated, two of the three industry definitions establish craftworker displacement.

Printing and publishing (SIC 27) data are the most aggregated and are available for the longest period of time. As a percent of total employment, craft workers declined from 25.6 percent in 1950 to 18.9 percent in 1980. This trend is summarized in Table 3.11. All three industry definitions indicate a dramatic decline in the proportion of compositors. This decline is offset largely by an increase in preparation and press craftsmen. The inverse trend in the proportional representations of composition and preparation/press craftsmen is indicated in Tables 3.11, 3.12, and 3.13.

As seen in Table 3.11, craft preparation and press employment as a percent of total industry (SIC 27) employment began to increase significantly after 1970. Within commercial printing (SIC 205) alone, Table 3.12 indicates that there has been a 2 percent increase in preparation and a 3.1 percent increase in press employment between 1970 and 1980. The proportional increase in preparation/press craftsmen was large enough to offset the decline of compositors. As a result of this offset, total commercial printing industry craft employment increased by 0.5 percent between 1970 and 1980. This trend is evidenced in Table 3.12.

Proportional craft employment declined significantly in the competitive labor market that includes commercial as well as in-plant and quick printers. Table 3.13 indicates that craft workers declined from 20 percent to 16 percent of all production workers between 1970 and 1980. Together, Tables 3.10 and 3.13 show the absolute and relative increase of in-plant and quick printing employment, as well as the shift of print-

Table 3.11: Craft Employment Printing and Publishing Industry, SIC 27, Selected Years 1950–90 (*percent of total employment*)

Occupation	1950	1960	1970	1980	1990
Compositors and Typesetters	17.0	13.1	10.3	5.9	6.2
Preparation and Press Operators	5.2	5.8	9.9	10.7	11.1
Bookbinders	3.4	2.3	2.6	2.3	2.4
Total Printing Craft Employment	25.6	21.2	22.8	18.9	19.7

Source: Compiled by the author.

Table 3.12: Craft Employment, Commercial Printing Industry, SIC 275, 1970 and 1980 *(percent of total employment)*

Occupation	1970	1980	Without Color Increase
Compositors and Typesetters	8.6	4.4	4.4
Preparation	5.9	7.9	6.4*
Press Operators	13.9	17.0	14.7*
Bookbinders	2.4	2.0	2.0
Total Craft Employment	30.8	31.3	27.5

Source: Compiled by the author.
* Estimate
Note: Proportional occupational employment data for industry SIC 27 and 275 are comparable to the total industry employment figures published by the Bureau of Labor Statistics in *Employment and Earnings in the United States: 1909-1978.*

Table 3.13: Competitive Labor Market to Craft Employment, 1970 and 1980 *(production workers)*

Occupation	1970		With Color Increase		Without Color Increase	
Typesetters	31,450	(5.8%)	18,480	(2.3%)	18,480	(2.4%)
Preparation	18,880	(3.5%)	32,840	(4.1%)	26,477	(3.4%)
Press Operators	49,000	(9.0%)	70,650	(8.8%)	60,814	(7.7%)
Bookbinders	8,560	(1.6%)	8,140	(1.0%)	8,140	(1.0%)
Total Craft	107,890	(19.9%)	130,110	(16.2%)	113,911	(14.5%)
Non-Craft	434,460	(80.1%)	671,567	(83.8%)	671,647	(85.5%)
Total Labor	542,350	(100%)	801,677	(100%)	785,558	(100%)

Source: Compiled by the author.

In terms of production workers, the competitive labor market in Table 3.13 is composed of:

Industry	1970	1980
Commercial Printing (SIC 275)	274,600	307,300
In-plant Printers	265,160	469,883
Quick Printers	2,590	24,494
Total Production Employment	542,350	801,677

ing production away from traditional processes and commercial printing industry boundaries. Using a different measure, Table 3.14 indicates that craft employment, as a percent of total competitive employment, declined from 15.2 to 12.1 percent in the same ten-year period.

Without correcting for the increase in craft-intensive color printing, proportional employment data obscures the continuing skilled worker displacement of new production technologies. In order to determine the magnitude of this increase in craftworkers explained by full color, the production index (Table 3.7) of full color shipments is used as a proxy to determine the distribution of employment growth between color and noncolor printing. Using commercial printing production index values to explain the growth in skilled employment requires two simplifying assumptions. First, during the period 1970–80 it is assumed that the proportion of craft labor per unit of production is constant for both color and noncolor printed matter. Second, it is assumed that on average, color printing accounted for a constant 45.5 percent during the ten years after 1970. Industry expert Coulson confirms the reasonableness of the first assumption but estimates that color work actually increased from 41 to 50 percent between 1970 and 1980. In order to determine the proportion of craft employment that color printing explains, full-color printing values are weighted by 45.5 percent and divided by the increase in the total index values. The increase in (Table 3.7) production index values attributable to color printing is 71.10 (.455/43.5), or 74 percent.[48]

If an accurate measure is used to determine the variation in craft occupational employment without the growth in full-color printing, then 74 percent of the growth in preparation and press craftworker employment during the same ten-year period is explained by color work. The bracketing occupations of composition and bookbinders are not significantly affected by color work. Removing 74 percent of the increase in preparation and press craftworker employment, Table 3.12 indicates that total craft employment, as a percent of total SIC 275 employment, declined from 30.8 to 27.5 percent between 1970 and 1980. Table 3.13 indicates that in the larger competitive market, craft employment declined from 20 to 14.5 percent of production workers.

More detailed and specific occupational titles were combined into the four main craft categories of compositor, combination preparation worker, pressman, and bookbinder to permit comparisons with training data. The category of compositor included the occupations of copy maker, hand compositor, imposer and make-up arranger, linecasting machine operator, linecasting machine keyboard operator, Ludlow machine operator, linotype casting machine operator, proofreader, composed copy, paste-up, and phototypesetting.

The titles included as craft compositor imply journeyman training. Two excluded composing room titles of linecasting machine tender and proof press operator are rarely manned by full journeymen and are classified as semiskilled.

The category of pressman includes letterpress operator and offset press operator. The job titles of press assistant and feeder are semi-skilled occupations which also probably included a residual number of unskilled pressroom workers.

Craft bookbinders include the job titles of hand bookbinder, cutter, and bindery machine setter. Semiskilled job titles include assembly, stitching, mailers, and all other bindery workers, operators, and semi-skilled workers. Unskilled bindery workers are included in the job title "all other laborers and nonskilled workers."

CRAFT DECLINE AND PRINTERS' RELATIVE WAGES

It is hypothesized that the decline in the level of craft skill between 1969 and 1982 led to the reduction in printers' earnings relative to those of manufacturing workers in general. In analyzing the effects of a decline in skill requirements on printers' wages, it is expected that such declines will cause a reduction in printing wages relative to those of workers as a whole. This relative printing wage hypothesis is tested by comparing a time series of printers' earnings with earnings of all manufacturing workers. It is anticipated that there will be a simultaneous decline in the printing craft skill index and printers' relative hourly earnings.

The measure of production worker average hourly earnings includes both skilled and semiskilled labor. Since the intention is to measure the impact of skill reduction on printers' relative earnings, a significant decline in the proportion of skilled production workers in either commercial printing (SIC 275) or manufacturing would explain a reduction in relative printers' wages. Data developed by the Bureau of the Census and presented in Table 3.14 indicate that the proportion of skilled, or craft, labor remained constant between 1970 and 1980. Craft occupational employment expressed as a percentage of total manufacturing employment declined by 1.6 percent to 27.7 percent between 1970 and 1980. Commercial printing industry craft employment increased slightly: from 30.8 percent in 1970 to 31.3 percent in 1980. (See Table 3.14).

Table 3.14: Craft Employment in Commercial Printing (SIC 275), Competitive Labor Market, Printing and Publishing (SIC 27), and Manufacturing (SIC Division D), 1960-80 *(percent of total employment)*

Year	Commercial Printing SIC 275	Competitive Labor Market	Printing And Publishing SIC 27	Manufacturing SIC Division D
1960	NA	NA	21.2	NA
1970	30.8	15.2	22.8	29.3
1980	31.3	12.1	18.9	27.7

Source: Compiled by the author.

In terms of total employment, the competitive labor market in Table 3.14 is composed of:

Industry	1970	1980
Commercial Printing (SIC 275)	354,200	413,700
In-plant Printers	352,662	624,944
Quick Printers	3,445	32,577
Total Employment	710,307	1,071,221

Total craftworker employment is 107,890 in 1970 and 130,110 in 1980 without eliminating the increase in skill-intensive full color printing employment.

The historical trend in relative printing production hourly earnings declining from 1.17 to 1.06 between 1968 and 1983 supports the hypothesis that skill reducing technology reduces relative printing wages since 1969. However, Table 3.15 understates the decline in printers' relative earnings. Indeed, if either the 3.8 percent increase in 1970–80 craft employment due to the incremental color printing demand (Table 3.12), or if the industry is defined in terms of competition, printers' relative earnings would decline even more significantly.

The relation between the decline in printers' skill and relative printing wages is also suggested in Table 3.15. During the last 25 years, the decline in printers' relative hourly earnings began only after the reduction in the craft skill index value in 1969. In the ten years prior to the decline in the craft skill index, printers' relative earnings are constant. The significant declines in printers' relative earnings and skill index value between 1969 and 1978 are caused by the reduction in the number of years' training required by nonunion printing industry craftsmen (Table 3.2). The reduction in the number of years in craft

Table 3.15: Chronological Relation of New Process Introduction, Printers' Craft Skill Index Value, and Printers' Relative Hourly Earnings, 1958–83.

Year	New Process Introduction	Craft Skill Index Value	Printer's Relative Hourly Earnings
1958		NA	1.17
1959	Electrophotography	NA	1.17
1960*		NA	1.17
1961		NA	1.17
1962		NA	1.17
1963	Photo-Direct Offset	NA	1.17
1964		NA	1.17
1965		NA	1.17
1966		5.81	1.17
1967	Digital CRT Typesetter	5.80	1.17
1968		5.80	1.16
1969		4.51	1.17
1970		3.54	1.19
1971		3.54	1.19
1972		3.52	1.20
1973		3.53	1.18
1974		3.47	1.16
1975		3.49	1.12
1976		3.48	1.11
1977		3.49	1.09
1978		3.47	1.09
1979		3.47	1.07
1980		3.45	1.08
1981		NA	1.07
1982		NA	1.06
1983		NA	1.06

Source: Compiled by the author.

*Systems to automatically develop and expose prepress materials, and to control color intensity and press register were continually introduced in the 1960's.

training is registered in the craft skill index. Each successive annual index value is calculated by multiplying the number of years of training required by the comparable percent of industry occupational employment and thereby reflects this decline. In 1969, for example, preparation and press craftsmen declined to four years from six years in 1968. Also as indicated in this table, typesetting apprenticeship in 1970 declined from six to four years in hot metal and from one and one-half to one year in cold composition. In addition to the influence of color printing, the decline in printer's relative earnings is understated since electrostatic and copy-to-plate processes, which entirely displaced craftworkers, are seldom employed within the narrowly defined commercial printing industry (SIC 225) market.

The interval between the decline in craft skill index and printers' relative earnings is caused by a lag in the diffusion of production innovations. The number of years' training, and hence the skill index, varies with the requirements of changing technology. In preparation and press functions, which employ more than two-thirds of industry craftsmen, union apprenticeship programs require training on new processes not generally available in participating plants. For example, all local union apprentices are required to attend the New York School of Printing to supplement their on-the-job training within the plant.[49]

The skill index decline for 1969 (Table 3.15) registers the influence of photocomposition, as well as the mechanization of hand operations and use of automatic controls on preparation and press equipment. The single most important influence of the skill index decline for 1969 is the introduction of photocomposition. This permitted the substitution of operators with one year of training for the hot metal craftsman with traditionally four years of training. This is indicated in Table 3.2. The surprisingly small interval between the first shipment of third generation photocomposition equipment in 1967 and the decline by 1969 of the training requirements caused by the more elementary elecromechanical and direct entry photocomposition devices which began to displace hot metal in the early 1960s.[50]

The measure of commercial printing industry production worker earnings includes a significant decline in the proportion of higher paid union printers. Instead of measuring both a decline in the level of craft and increased proportion of unskilled labor, it can be argued that variation in relative earnings only registers the decline in labor market unionization. While national nonunion industry wage data is not available, such data is available for craft workers in New York City for 1958–82. Table 3.16 measures the historical variation in New York City skilled nonunion printing production workers' relative earnings. It is expected that there will be a simultaneous decline in the number of years' training as well as the nonunion skilled printers relative hourly earnings.

The historical trend of the relative earnings of skilled, nonunion printers in New York City is consistent with the variation in total printing industry production workers. Table 3.16 separately measures the trend in the relative earnings of skilled, nonunion printers and is a more direct measure of the influence of craft decline on skilled printing wages. There is a continuation of the increase in relative craft wages before the reduction in apprenticeship training. The number of years of craft training required, as well as the printers' skill index, both begin to

Table 3.16: Chronological Relation of Number of Years' Training, and Ratio of Skilled Nonunion Printing Production Hourly Wage Rate to Average Hourly Earnings of all Manufacturing Production Workers in New York City, 1958–82

Year	Typesetting (Hot)		Preparation		Press		Bindery	
	Years	Ratio	Years	Ratio	Years	Ratio	Years	Ratio
1958	6	1.45	6	1.49	6	1.47	5	1.26
1959	6	1.48	6	1.51	6	1.50	5	1.30
1960	6	1.47	6	1.51	6	1.49	5	1.33
1961	6	1.47	6	1.49	6	1.47	5	1.34
1962	6	NA	6	NA	6	NA	5	NA
1963	6	1.50	6	1.48	6	1.46	5	1.33
1964	6	1.50	6	1.49	6	1.47	5	1.37
1965	6	1.53	6	1.51	6	1.44	5	1.39
1966	6	1.52	6	1.49	6	1.43	5	1.38
1967	6	1.56	6	1.52	6	1.47	5	1.48
1968	6	1.57	6	1.50	6	1.44	5	1.47
1969	6	1.60	4	1.48	4	1.44	5	1.50
1970	4	1.62	4	1.61	3	1.54	5	1.53
1971	4	1.64	4	1.63	3	1.56	5	1.54
1972	4	1.63	4	1.61	3	1.55	5	1.53
1973	4	NA	4	NA	3	NA	5	NA
1974	4	1.72	4	1.65	3	1.58	5	1.61
1975	4	1.75	4	1.63	3	1.58	5	1.64
1976	4	1.72	4	1.66	3	1.58	5	1.62
1977	4	1.71	4	1.64	3	1.58	5	1.60
1978	4	1.68	4	1.62	3	1.55	5	1.58
1979	4	1.65	4	1.51	3	1.52	5	1.54
1980	4	1.63	4	1.39	3	1.50	5	1.53
1981	4	1.62	4	1.30	3	1.50	5	1.52
1982	4	1.61	4	1.22	3	1.48	5	1.51

Source: Compiled by the author.

Note: Cold typesetting wage rates are not available according to Richard Anderson, executive vice-president, Master Printers' Section, in a telephone interview on 16 August, 1983.

decline in 1969. Nationwide, printers' relative earnings begin to decline in that year. In New York City, these wages begin their decline in 1975–76. The interval between the decline in training and relative earnings in 1969 is four years for all industry workers and six to seven years for those nonunion craftworkers in New York City.

Parallel movement of four craft wage rates in Table 3.16 suggests that institutional factors are mediating the influence of skill upon relative wages. In 1975, relative nonunion wage rates of craft workers in typesetting, preparation, press, and bindery began their eight-year decline. Bookbinders, the only craft that did not experience a decline in the number of years' training, also experienced a decline in their relative earnings. While comprising only 2 percent of total industry employment (see Table 3.3), the decline in relative bindery wages does not follow the length of craft training.

Expert opinion suggests that the movement of relative wages in New York City reflects an aggregate variation in skill. In a joint interview with the respective directors of the union and nonunion employment associations in New York, Anderson and Horne stated that there has been a deliberate effort to maintain relative wages between craftworkers in each of the four functions. Employer and employee resistance to intercraft wage variation mediates the influence of skill decline in a particular craft. This suggests that nonunion craft wage variation in New York City in Table 3.16 is only a rough measure of the aggregate decline in printing skills.[51]

SUMMARY

Chapter 3 establishes that new production technology reduces the level of skill required in printing production. Evidence of the historic decline in printing skill is found in variations in training requirements (Table 3.2), craft skill index (Table 3.4), as well as the decline of printers relative earnings (Tables 3.15, 3.16). The hypothesis of deskilling is further supported by the reduction in the proportional employment of craft workers in the competitive labor market between 1970 and 1980 (Table 3.13) despite the increase in skill-intensive color printing.

NOTES

1. Printing Industries of Metropolitan New York, Inc., Master Printers' Section, "Recommended Standards of Wages and Hours," 1965; and U. S. Department of Labor, Bureau of Apprenticeship and Training, "National Apprenticeship and Training Standards for the Graphic Arts International Union" (Employment and Training Administration, 1981), p. 6.

2. U. S. Department of Labor. Bureau of Labor Statistics. *Employment Outlook in Printing Occupations,* bulletin 1126 (Washington, DC: GPO, 1951), 304 (hereafter cited as *Employment Outlook),* and E. W. Andrews, *Employment Trends in the Printing Trades* (Chicago: Science Research Associated, 1939), 42 (hereafter cited as *Employment Trends).*

3. Jack Simick. Telephone interview with the author, 15 September 1983 (hereafter as Simich 9/15).

4. "Contract for Book and Job Work Between Printers' League Section, Printing Industries of Metropolitan New York, Inc., and New York Typographical Union No. 6,"

(1955–57): 5–6 (hereafter cited as "Metropolitan, 1955–57"), and Union Employers of America, "The Future," 8.

5.   Barnett, *Chapters*, 162, and Andrews, *Employment Trends*, 42.

6.   Metropolitan, (1974–75), 82; "Contract for Book and Job Offices Between Print-ers' League Section, Printing Industries of Metropolitan New York, Inc. and Graphic Arts International Union, No. 119B," (1976–78): 35, (hereafter cited as "119B, [1976–78]"); "Contract for Book and Job Offices Between Printers' League Section, Printing Industries of Metropolitan New York, Inc. and Printing and Graphic Communications Union, No. 51. IP & GCU—AFL–CIO" (1977–78): 59, (hereafter cited as "51, [1977–78]").

7.   Richard Anderson. Interview with the author, 7 April 1983. Anderson is executive vice-president, Master Printers' Section of the Printing Industries of Metropolitan New York, Inc. (hereafter cited as Anderson, 4/83).

8.   "Contract for Book and Job Work Between Printers' League Section, Printing Industries of Metropolitan New York, Inc. and New York Typographical Union No. 6" (1974–75): 60, 67, 82, 86 (hereafter cited as "Metropolitan, (1974–75)," and Richard Anderson and James E. Horne, joint interview, 24 August, 1983. Anderson and Horne are the executive vice-presidents of the respective nonunion and union employer associations of the Printing Industries of Metropolitan New York, Inc.

9.   James E. Horne. Personal correspondence with the author, 16 April 1985 (hereafter cited as Horne, 4/85).

10.   Jack Simich. Telephone interview with the author, 28 June 1983 (hereafter cited as Simich, 6/28); Dennis Molloy. Telephone interview with the author, 6 May 1983. Molloy is vice-president, Graphic Arts Employers of America. (Hereafter cited as Molloy, 5/6); and James E. Horne. Telephone Interview with the author, 28 June 1983 (hereafter cited as Horne, 6/28).

11.   George Silvestri, Division of Occupational and Administrative Statistics, Bureau of Labor Statistics, U. S. Department of Labor. Telephone interview with the author, 28 December 1983, (hereafter cited as Silvestri, 12/28), and U. S. Department of Labor, Bureau of Labor Statistics, *Occupational Employment in the Commercial Printing Industry, March 1970*, (Washington, DC, 1970) 5.

12.   Strauss, *Printing*, 149. Comparative cost data for full color and nonfull color are available from the Porte Publishing Company. Porte annually publishes national unit price data which are often used in pricing of printed matter.

13.   Michael G. Coulson, "Global Influences of the Graphic Arts" *Market Research Newsletter*, (October 1984): 1–2, (hereafter cited as "Global Influences"). The *Market Research Newsletter* is a publication of the GATF.

14.   GATF. *Forecast 8*, 3, 63–4.

15.   U. S. Department of Labor, Wages and Hours Division. *Economic Factors Bear-ing on Minimum Wages in the Printing and Publishing and Allied Graphic Arts Indus-try* (Washington, DC: GPO, 1942), 40 (hereafter cited as *Factors Bearing on Minimum Wages*).

16.   GATF, *Niche No. 1 Report*, 11–12; and Bruno, 8/24.

17.   Battelle Columbus Division. *Interaction of Markets and Technology on Graphic Communication: 1980-1985 Expectations and Opportunities*, (Arlington, VA: Printing Industries of America, 1980), 136 (hereafter cited as *Interaction of Markets*).

18.   U. S. Department of Commerce. Bureau of the Census. *Standard Industrial Classification Manual*, (Washington, DC: GPO, 1972), 106–11.

19.   Jack Simich. Telephone interview with the author, 30 June 1983 (hereafter cited as Simich, 6/30); Daniels, 9/30; Cook, 4/6; and DeMinco, 12/8.

20.   National Association of Printers and Lithographers. "How Developments in Reproduction Technology Are Affecting Markets," NAPL Special Report (Teaneck, NJ:

National Association of Printers and Lithographers, 1983), 4; Daniels, 9/30; Brian S. Cook. Personal correspondence with the author, 30 March 1984 (hereafter cited as Cook, 3/30); Frank J. Romano, *Printing Industry Trends Almanac* (Arlington, VA: Printing Industries of America, 1980), 21 (hereafter cited as *Industry Trends);* and Eastman-Kodak Company. *Manpower,* 7, 25.

21.   J. Llamas. Telephone interview with the author, 22 July 1983. Llamas is vice president of the In-Plant Management Association, New Orleans, LA (hereafter cited as Llamas, 7/22); and Robert Baker. Telephone interview with the author, 1 July 1983. Baker is president of the In-Plant Management Association, New Orleans, LA (hereafter cited as Baker, 7/1); and Battelle Columbus Division. *Interaction of Markets,* 137–8.

22.   Michael Bruno. Telephone interview with the author, 24 August 1983. Bruno is editor and publisher, *What's New In Graphic Communications?* Nashua, NH (hereafter cited as Bruno, 8/24); and Baker, 7/1.

23.   GATF. *Niche No. 1 Report,* 13, 26, 30.

24.   Munson, *Labor Relations,* 52.

25.   John Trieste. Interview with the author, 24 August 1983 (hereafter cited as Trieste, 8/24).

26.   Strauss, *Printing,* 148.

27.   Strauss, *Printing,* 148–50.

28.   Strauss, *Printing,* 149, 158–61; Munson, *Labor Relations,* 74–5; Michael G. Coulson. Telephone interview with the author, 12 April 1985. Coulson is senior marketing research analyst, Graphic Arts Technical Foundation (hereafter cited as Coulson, 4/12); Michael Chazin and Elizabeth G. Berglund, "Color Separation Systems," *Inland/Printer Lithographer,* (September 1978): 45; and International Paper Company. *Pocket Pal* (New York: International Paper Company, 1979), 183, 190–1.

29.   Xerox Corporation. "Xerox Fact," 19; R. M. Scharfert, "Electrophotography Yesterday, Today and Tomorrow," *Photographic Science and Engineering,* 22(3):152 (hereafter cited as "Electrophotography"); and William Lamparte. Telephone interview with the author 13 October 1983. Lamparte is consultant, National Association of Printers and Lithographers (hereafter cited as Lamparte, 10/13).

30.   GATF. *Techno-Economic Forecast 8: The Future of Color Printing, 1979–1983,* (Pittsburgh, PA: GATF, 1978), 183 (hereafter cited as *Forecast 8).*

31.   GATF. *Forecast 9,* 350–1; William H. Bureau, "Copying/Duplicating Methods Through the Years," *Graphic Arts Monthly* (December 1977): 77–9 (hereafter cited as "Copying/Duplicating"); Friday, *Quick Printing,* 350–1; and Klasnic, *Inplant,* 147–8.

32.   Britt, "Upheaval," 28; Friday, *Quick Printing,* 366–7; Klasnic, *Inplant,* 142–9; and "No Matter What You Publish or Print—Copiers Are Gaining on You," *Vectors* (January 1984): 1.

33.   GATF. *Niche No. 1 Report* (Pittsburgh, PA: 1983), 30.

34.   GATF. *Niche No. 1 Report,* 5–7, 25; and GATF. *Forecast 8,* 105–7, 162, 183.

35.   Robert L. Schweiger, letter of 31 August, 1983.

36.   Donald Piercy, "Today's Quick Printers Are Tomorrow's Commercial Printers," *Quick Printing,* 7(4): 36 (hereafter cited as Today's Quick Printers").

37.   GATF. *Niche No. 1 Report,* 506.

38.   U. S. Department of Labor. Wages and Hours Division. *Factors Bearing on Minimum Wages,* 20; Donald Piercy. Telephone interview with the author, 13 July 1983. Piercy is president, American Quick Printers Association, Houston, TX (hereafter cited as Piercy, 7/13); and Battelle Columbus Division, *Interaction of Markets,* 137–8.

39.   Eastman-Kodak Company, *Manpower,* 273; and GATF, *Forecast 9,* 8.

40.   U.S. Department of Commerce. *Standard Industrial Classification Manual* (Washington, DC: GPO, 1972), 107–8, and U.S. Department of Labor. *Employment and Earnings,* 615–32.

41. U.S. Department of Labor. Bureau of Labor Statistics. *Employment and Earnings in the United States, 1909–1978,* (Washington, DC: GPO, 1978) pp 52–3, 615–32.

42. Mr. Charles R. Cook. Telephone interview with the author, 20 July, 1983. Cook is acting director, forest products, Printing and Packaging Division, Office of Basic Industries, Bureau of Industrial Economics, U.S. Department of Commerce, (hereafter cited as Cook, 7/20).

43. GATF, *Niche No. 1, Report 3.*

44. International Resource Development, Inc., *In-Plant Printing in the Age of Corporate Electronic Publishing,* Report 613 (Norwalk, CT.: International Resource Development, 1984), 21, 42–3.

45. Ford Ray, telephone interview with author, May 8, 1985; and Michael Coulson, Graphic Arts Technical Foundation, telephone interview with the author May 10, 1985.

46. Donald Ramstad. Telephone interview with the author, 25 July, 1983. Ramstad is national accounts sales manager, 3M Company (hereafter cited as Ramstad, 7/25).

47. Ramstad, 7/25.

48. Michael G. Coulson. Telephone Interview with author, October 24, 1985. Mr. Coulson, in a letter dated May 24, 1984, developed the historical production index of full-color, noncolor, and total commercial printing industry shipments (1967–84).

49. *Standards of Apprenticeship for Pressmen,* Joint Negotiating Committee of the Printers' League Section and New York Printing Pressmen's Union, No. 51, April 1, 1953: 8; 51, (1977-1978): 59.

50. L. W. Wallis, *Electronic Typesetting* (Gateshead, UK: Paradigam Press, 1984), 127.

51. James E. Horne. Interview with the author, 7 April 1983 (hereafter cited as Horne, 4/83); and Anderson, 4/83.

4

Craft Union
Response to
Technological Change

INTRODUCTION

Chapter 4 which analyzes the influence upon membership of several trade union responses to skill displacement, begins by presenting three historical craft union responses which may have either a positive or negative influence upon union membership. These three responses are: work rules, the expansion of union membership to include the unskilled, and the recruitment of nonunion printers. The existence and influence of each union policy shall be examined in industry collective bargaining agreements, union leadership statements, expert opinion, and relative wage data.

Two union policies identify the potential for increasing union membership: the consolidation of single-craft unions into industrial organizations, and the recruitment of competitive labor into the ranks of union membership. The chapter evaluates the purpose and success of these two trade union policies for organizing unskilled labor on the basis of trade literature and National Labor Relations Board (NLRB) representation data.

In addition to craft decline, the union membership model hypothesizes that work rules are the second cause of the decline in the membership of the ITU and GCIU. Despite the historical potential of increasing union membership through the expansion of eligibility to the unskilled, as well as recruitment of new members, the chapter isolates the dominating influence of work rules in the decline in membership by comparing the proportion of union operators before and after the introduction of new technology.

This chapter also tests the two hypotheses concerning the consequence of union work rules. It is hypothesized that the ITU and GCIU maintained relative skilled membership wages in response to a decline in the level of printing craftworkers skills. Second, it is hypothesized that in response to complete skill displacement, the ITU and GCIU increased relative union/nonunion new process wage rates. In the case of occupational skill decline, if the union skilled wage is constant relative to nonunion workers in general, then it is expected that union employment will decline.

This chapter ends with a review of two works that isolate a third variable, management behavior, as a determinant of union membership. First, the general theory of work place transformation, as set forth in *Segmented Work, Divided Workers* by Gordon, Edwards, and Reich, will be applied to the printing industry. Subsequently, the chapter reviews Gregory Geibel's article entitled "Corporate Structure, Technology and the Printing Industry" to consider the independent contribution of both changes in corporate structure and the outmigration of firms from traditional printing centers as causes of union membership decline.

INDUSTRIAL UNION STRUCTURE

With the decline of craft orientation, industrial unions began to recruit members from throughout the entire printing process, rather than from only a particular production stage. Moreover, in response to technological change, union organization is accelerated by the merger of craft unions. Between 1958 and 1983, as indicated below in Table 5.1, the ten commercial printing craft unions merged into four larger unions. These unions, in turn, included in their membership workers from more than one, if not all, stages of production. With the merger of the pressmen and bindery unions on 1 July 1983, only two major AFL-CIO unions remained: the GCIU and the ITU. There are two advantages to this process of merger and consolidation: broader plant and company-wide jurisdiction.

Broader Plant Jurisdiction

The creation of broader plant jurisdiction through mergers increases union power to maintain both employment and relative wages in existing shops. Technology, union leaders argue, is erasing the distinctive jurisdictions of the traditionally separate craft skills. Instead of craft jurisdictional disputes, consolidation of craft unions would provide increased bargaining power at the plant level. In addition, it would provide membership with greater job mobility and security in the face of technological change.

Published statements by the presidents of the GCIU and ITU indicate that industrial organization would permit the printing union to better respond to the threat to technology and new corporate structures in previously unionized shops. Union leaders argue that reorganization will also provide the combined resources necessary to organize the fast growing nonunion printing industry.

The GCIU indicates that industrial unionism is a response to "technology and the growth of conglomerates in the industry."[1] A clear statement of purpose was made after the merger in 1983 of the pressmen and bindery unions in the *Union Tabloid*.

> North America's largest graphic arts union ever—the Graphic Communications International Union (GCIU)—brings a whole new perspective and horizon as it ends 75 years of bitter jurisdictional conflicts. The united union intentions from Day One is to concentrate on preserving job security and contract benefits in the face of revolutionary new technological developments now and coming into the printing industry.
>
> It will mobilize the strength necessary to confront the restructured and powerful corporate and conglomerate ownership in today's graphic arts.
>
> A top emphasis, as part of achieving this, will be a broader organizing effort than ever before to bring unionism to the fast growing non-union segment.[2]

International Typographical Union President Bevis, in his opening address to the 119th Convention of the ITU, stated: "We can no longer continue to operate on the basis of a purely craft union. It is essential that we move toward an industrial type of union structure." Four years later, during his own term in office, ITU President Bingel attributed the erosion of members' jobs and security to the technological revolution in the printing industry.[3]

Unified bargaining, it is felt, will strengthen the union within the previously organized shops. In 1973, Kenneth J. Brown, president of the then-named Graphic Arts Union International, indicated that the broader jurisdiction of industrial unions would eliminate craft jurisdictional disputes created by new processes. Technology would serve to merge the functions of the various crafts.

The Graphic Arts Union International has been operating since September 4. As you know, we represent the lithographers, photoengravers and bookbinders. For the first time you have a union in the graphic arts that is in a position to represent people in the plant from the front door to the back door. One of the things that has plagued the industry over the years has been the fragmentation of the unions. We were process oriented. We thought in terms of our skills and consequently there was competition between the unions. Occasionally, as technological development began to change, the industry and management were affronted with several unions making conflicting demands in the course of the year, this often led to interruptions in production that we can now say were perhaps unnecessary.[4]

One example of a jurisdictional conflict is the existing dispute between the GCIU and the ITU. John J. Pilch, president of the ITU, agrees with other labor leaders that union mergers are the solution to craft jurisdictional problems. In 1971, however, Mr. Pilch claimed part of the pressmen's jurisdiction. Today, in response to skill displacement, the ITU takes the position it held in the days when it was the only graphic arts union: it claims that it still has absolute jurisdiction over all prepress operations. According to Pilch:

A basic question lies in the area of page make-up. The ITU's original jurisdiction was all the work necessary to get an object on press. We still feel that the other unions have backed into our area. When new presses came in and brought stereotypers we still did all the work to give stereotypers material to make duplicate plates. With the conversion to offset, stereotypers are no longer necessary.[5]

Broader jurisdiction also provides members with greater mobility between functions and hence greater job security. Union President Brown stated the advantages of removing unnecessary jurisdictional distinctions after the merger of the photoengravers and lithographers in 1964. After the success of this merger became apparent, Brown states that "as a result of the merger we have been able to move men with comparable skills across what used to be arbitrary union lines."[6] Broader jurisdiction has provided the printing unions with the opportunity to promote the movement of workers from technologically affected branches of the trade to those still unaffected. It should be noted here that Barnett also concludes that just such a mobility within the trade was the most effective way of checking inflow into the trade and of preserving job opportunities for displaced skills.[7]

The development from craft to industrial-type union organization consolidates the remaining power of industry unions and provides the union with a response to the technological convergence of the various printing functions. Industrial organization, however, has had an uneven effect on both the union and the nonunion segments of the printing industry. Unions with broader jurisdiction have strengthened their control over organized shops and have, as a result, provided their members with high relative wages as well as potentially greater mobility and job security. With broader jurisdiction, printers can negotiate with a more unified, powerful strike threat.

Company-Wide Jurisdiction

By increasing union power over existing plants, an industrial structure gives printers the opportunity to define jurisdiction in terms of plant ownership rather than locality. Defining jurisdiction in such terms prevents owners and employers from relocating plants outside union jurisdiction. Company-wide jurisdiction specifically allows printing unions to address problems caused by multiple plant ownership and the increasing regional mobility of printing plants.

Perhaps the first contract to eliminate geographical boundaries was the agreement made in 1967 between Local No. 6 of the ITU and Printers League Section of the Printing Industries of Metropolitan New York, Inc. While rare even in 1983, this precedent-setting contract created a company boundary rather than a regional one.[8] The language governing this part of the agreement was developed in response to plant relocations from New York City. Signed on 22 October 1967, this contract's language has been effective in retaining the jurisdicton of Local No. 6 over many relocated plants. This contract language reads:

> In the event of the removal of any plant covered by this Contract to a location outside the geographical jurisdiction of New York Typographical Union No. 6, the employer shall continue to recognize New York Typographical Union No. 6 as the bargaining agent for its composing room employees and this Contract shall continue to apply.[9]

The mobility of a typical printing plant is limited to the local market it serves. Traditionally, printing plants were local, which in turn causes both employers and craft unions to organize themselves on a local basis. The local market orientation is evidenced by a Bureau of the Census survey of transportation patterns exhibited by 1,216 printing and publishing establishments. In 1967, for example, the survey found that 43 percent of all commercial printing shipments were made to customers less than 50 miles away.[10]

Bindery Union President Brown, as well as Pressmen's Union President Rohan, conclude that industrial unionism permits union leadership to deal more effectively with increased plant mobility and mulitiple plant ownership in particular. While evidence, as demonstrated in a later section, does not support the several theories presented in regard to increased ownership concentration or multiple plant operations, there is evidence of plant mobility within certain printing product markets.[11]

ORGANIZATION OF NEW MEMBERSHIP

In addition to strengthening its power over existing union plants, the unified strength of merged unions is intended to increase their effectiveness in organizing nonunion printers. Evidence of this sentiment is found in a statement by Kenneth J. Rohan during a merger negotiation in 1974. He states that "the objective of merger is to mobilize our forces so as to more effectively organize the non-union segment of the industry. And we are doing it."[12]

This objective was again stated in 1973. After the merger of the printing and bindery unions, the *Union Tabloid* predicted that a major emphasis would be placed on organizing the fast growing nonunion segment of the industry.[13]

Consistently, the leadership of the GCIU has stated that they have given priority to organizing nonunion workers. Yet, the GCIU, which represented approximately 80 percent of the printing industry union membership as of 1981, dedicated a surprisingly small portion of its budget to plant organizational efforts. In 1980, for example, the two component unions of the GCIU voted to establish a 50 cent per month per capita organizing fund for their combined memberships which then totaled 167,000. The annualized membership assessment of approximately $1,000,000 would be used to organize approximately 500,000 nonunion production workers in printing and publishing.[14]

Measurement of Union Organization Success

A measure of the success of union organizational activities is the number of NLRB representation elections won in the printing industry. Through victory in these elections, unions hope to gain recognition from the employer as the bargaining agent for his employees. Table 4.1 presents the results of NLRB representation elections between 1958 and 1981.[15]

Table 4.1: NLRB Representation Elections in the Printing, Publishing, and Allied Products Industries, 1958–81

Year	Total Elections	Elections in which Representation Rights Won by Unions						Elections in which No Representative Chosen	Employees Eligible To Vote	Valid Votes Cast
		Total	AFL–CIO	T	ONU	OLU	UU			
1958	150	108	92				16	47	4,147	3,771
1959	178	127	86				41	51	6,064	5,586
1960	228	148	90				58	80	7,080	6,378
1961	216	150	89				61	66	5,976	5,448
1962	293	198	120				78	95	7,233	6,645
1963	261	166	98				68	95	6,523	6,006
1964	242	148	87	7	51		3	94	8,784	8,094
1965	259	156	128	14	14			103	12,154	10,891
1966	271	157	128	15	11	3		114	9,901	9,024
1967	276	171	146	15	4	6		105	11,386	10,215
1968	305	178	153	12	11	2		127	12,734	11,507
1969	292	155	134	11	3	7		137	12,849	11,704
1970	297	160	131	16	4	9		137	10,900	9,583
1971	290	150	110	25	6	9		140	11,253	10,285
1972	292	159	141	13	5	10		133	9,858	8,971
1973	327	167	143	16	3	5		160	10,537	9,459
1974	320	159	138	13	2	6		161	12,977	11,776
1975	297	144	118	13	4	9		153	10,400	9,389
1976	263	134	103	12	6	13		129	11,971	10,597
1977	319	143	111	24	1	7		176	15,086	13,449
1978	262	123	102	7	3	11		139	13,704	12,418
1979	263	90	75	11	2	2		173	12,888	11,716
1980	241	107	92	12		3		134	13,165	11,986
1981	209	89	72	11	1	5		120	12,008	10,374

Source: Bureau of National Affairs, Inc., Research and Special Projects Division. *Annual Report of the National Labor Relations Board* (Washington, DC: GPO, 1983).

Note: T=Teamsters; ONU=other national unions; OLU=other local unions; UU=unaffiliated unions.

Historical data for the NLRB indicate both that there exists a small proportion of industry employment where representation is contested, and that a declining number of such elections were won by unions. Production employment in the printing and publishing industry (SIC 27) increased from 563,200 to 699,300 in the years between 1958 and 1981. Despite this, the total number of employees eligible to vote as a result of this union organizing activity never exceeded 15,086. Most significant is the fact that representation elections won by all unions actually declined from 72 percent in 1958 to 43 percent in 1981. Without developing an effective organizational capability, perhaps this necessary condition for printing union survival will be lost.[16]

Expanded Labor Market Definition

Recognizing the increasingly unskilled nature of printing production, union leaders must focus their organizational efforts on an expanded labor supply as defined by competition. This competitive labor supply should include all substitute suppliers employing new, nonconventional printing processes. With the increasing capabilities of these processes, job opportunities will be lost to displaced memberships if union organization efforts are limited to traditional production processes.

The present union labor market definition is too narrow. The combined union definition of the competitive labor market is limited to printing and publishing (SIC 27) and paper and allied products (SIC 26). The ITU more narrowly defines its nonunion competitors as the "unorganized workers in the graphic arts industry." Given the traditional newspaper and commercial membership of the ITU, the organization target of the compositors would reasonably be the printing and publishing (SIC 27) production workers.[17]

Brown, who in 1983 became the president of the largest of the two remaining unions, described the labor market in terms of industry unions that would organize production workers in SIC 27 and SIC 26. During an interview in 1974, Brown stated:

> Specifically: there is nothing in the politics or plans of the unions to include clerical workers in our organization. . . . We are interested in adding employees to the graphic arts industry. The line we tend to draw is on people who are essentially involved in the production of the graphic arts and product as opposed to servicing that product.[18]

On the basis of various merger negotiations, "graphic arts" employees are defined to include the United Papermakers and Paperworkers Union (130,000 members as of 1974) and the ITU. With the exception of papermakers, all possible union membership would be confined to printing and publishing (SIC 27). In 1978, 90 percent of all paperworkers were employed in paper and allied products (SIC 26).[19]

The relative employment growth data shown in Table 3.7 indicate that union printers are losing their industry identity and market share to competitive suppliers and, in particular, to the growing number of in-plant printers. Despite their dramatic growth since 1958, GATF estimates captive plants have only penetrated one-half of their potential market. By altering the process, technology has expanded the range of environments and capabilities of nonprinters to provide substitute printed products. Through simplification in printing and typesetting, the printing and binding of small quantities of materials have become routine office functions on word processing and electrostatic printing equipment. Former large volume printing customers install photocomposition and duplicating equipment in their captive plants. Quick printers, with their convenient locations and quick turn-around on duplication, electrostatic, and photocomposition equipment, provide the consumer with an alternative to the commercial printer.[20]

THE JOURNEYMAN RULE

Definition and Purpose

Since the introduction of the linotype in the 1890s, printing unions have required that craftsmen operate any new equipment capable of performing the function of journeymen at rates of pay and terms of employment equal to those of journeymen themselves. The persistence of this rule is seen in the pressmen's and binders' agreements with the Printer's League Section, Printing Industries of Metropolitan New York, Inc. Expert industry opinion indicates that the language found in the New York contracts is representative of industry contracts throughout the United States.[21]

Industry Agreements and the ITU

In September 1955, Local No. 6 of the ITU signed a traditional industry agreement giving the union complete jurisdiction over new process equipment. This agreement also limited composing room work to journeymen and apprentices. With regard to all composition work, the agreement states that "Jurisdiction of the union is defined as including all composing room work in Book and Job shops covered by this contract. . . ."[22]

Union jurisdiction over all new processes and equipment is further crystallized in this statement:

> When any member of the League determines to install any new machinery, equipment or process, he shall notify the union of that

fact specifically describing it. ... It is recognized that a reasonable time of actual employment on such work is needed to attain proficiency. Only journeymen or apprentices in their fourth, fifth or sixth year of apprenticeship shall be employed on such work. In the event that the union is not able to supply such journeymen or apprentices, the Union shall supply other trained employees to perform the work at the schedule of wages herein provided in Section 3.[23]

The restriction of composing room work to craftsmen is specified in the "Jurisdiction" section of the same agreement:

The work of the composing room shall be performed only by apprentices and journeymen, but it is mutually agreed, notwithstanding the foregoing, that office boys (not apprentices) may carry proofs and copy, and sort and put away leads, furniture, cuts and plates, shall not set, make-up or distribute type, nor break up forms, nor act as bankmen.[24]

The Local No. 6 contract language of the agreement signed in January 1983 is nearly identical to that found in the agreement for 1955 with respect to union jurisdiction over all composing room and new process work. With the signing of the agreement of October 1975, the ITU recognized the semiskilled nature of some photocomposition work with the inclusion in the contract of a new job category, "Computer Typist." However, the duties of this job classification were so severely limited as to make the classification meaningless. Furthermore, until 1983, disputes among the employers prevented determination of a salary scale.[25]

Industry Agreements and the Printing Pressmen

The contract language of the agreement between the Printing Pressmen's Union (Local No. 51) and the Printer's League indicates that all preparation or press work on either old or new process equipment is to be considered within the local's jurisdiction. Within the pressroom, jurisdiction is defined in terms of sheet size, number of cylinders, and the method of feeding as outlined in contract sections entitled "Character of Work" and "Complement of Men." For the pressmen by 1957 new process jurisdiction meant jurisdiction over recently installed offset equipment. The contract for 1957, moreover, recognized Local No. 51 as the representative of all offset operations. Between this agreement and that signed in 1983, League contract language is very similar and has the effect of maintaining within the jurisdiction of Local

No. 51 all preparation and press work regardless of the process or equipment.

Except when specifically noted, all work within the pressmen's jurisdiction is presumed to be done by journeymen. Similar language in both the agreements for 1957 and 1983 regarding the "Character of Work" and "Complement of Men" indicates when an assistant is permitted to help a journeyman. The pressmen's contract requires that photo-direct offset equipment be operated by a press assistant with two and one-half years of apprenticeship training. The number of semi-skilled operators, or unskilled tenders helping a pressman, depends upon the number of cylinders, sheet size, and method of paper handling.[26]

Industry Agreements and Bindery Workers

The bindery workers' contract is very similar to the pressmen's contract. The jurisdiction of the New York Papercutters and Bookbinders Union (Local No. 119) is defined in terms of equipment rather than function but, in fact, covers all finishing work as specified in the contracts for 1958 and 1976. The control by Local No. 119 over new processes and its stipulation that displaced journeymen operate all new equipment is clear in the following contract language for 1984–86.

> In the event of the introduction of new processes or new technology, the employment and the compensation of men or other operators shall be settled by mutual agreement determined after a trial period mutually agreed upon. In the event that the introduction of new processes or machinery shall result in the displacement of an employee, an opportunity to man this equipment shall be afforded the displaced employee before any other employee is transferred to or hired for any such opening.[27]

Incremental Cost of the Journeyman Rule

This section estimates the incremental cost of the journeyman rule requiring the employment of a craftsman in an unskilled operation of photocomposition and small press work. This cost is estimated on the basis of New York City union and nonunion occupational hourly wage rates.

The incremental cost of employing a higher skilled union member to perform an unskilled new process operation is estimated by the ratio of the union journeyman wage to the nonunion wage for new process operation. Union and nonunion hourly wage rates are available for 1959 and 1982 from the Printing Industries of Metropolitan New York, Inc. Union hourly wage rates for journeyman compositors and the least skilled category of press operators, "assistant cylinder pressmen," are available from Local No. 6 of the ITU and Local No. 51 of the Pressmen's Union respectively.

Proxy wage rates for nonunion photocomposition and electrostatic operators are also required for this present analysis. Of the available wage data, the most comparable occupation to a photocomposition operator is a hand and machine bindery worker. The most appropriate proxy photocomposition wage rate is that of a word-processing operator. Word processing and photocomposition systems require similar typing and text manipulation ability. The classification of a bindery worker who independently operates stitching and drilling equipment in a production environment is comparable to that of a union photocomposition operator. In 1977, the wage scale of a nonunion bindery hand and machine operator exceeded by 16 percent that of a Class A Typist employed in a northeastern manufacturing industry. The nonunion "unskilled" helper is used at the electrostatic operator proxy wage rate because of the similarity of working environment and skill level. Nonunion occupational wage rates are available for the new process photodirect operator.[28]

Table 4.2 estimates that the journeyman rule more than doubled the hourly wage rate in both photocomposition and electrostatic equipment operation. Consistent with the relative cost of employing a union compositor in photocomposition is a comparison of the hourly wage of a journeyman and a Class A Typist. In 1977, journeymen in Local No. 6 were paid $11.24 per hour in photocomposition situations where a Class A Typist could have been employed for $4.44 per hour.[29]

The constant photo-direct offset and the declining electrostatic relative union/nonunion wage rates reflect a moderation in the wage demands of Local No. 51 of the Pressmen's Union. According to James E. Horne, the employer-representative of the New York Employer Association, the pressman's local introduced a lower wage rate for small

Table 4.2: **Ratio of Union Hourly Wage Costs Under Journeyman Rule to Hourly Wage Cost of Non-Union Labor in Photocomposition, Photo-Direct Offset and Electrostatic Processes, 1959 and 1982**

Year	Photocomposition	Photo-Direct Offset	Electrostatic
1959	2.13	1.53	2.73
1982	2.45	1.53	2.43

Source: Compiled by the author.

press equipment utilizing the photodirect process in order to stop the loss of jobs to nonunion plants. In contrast to earlier years, the Local No. 51 contract for 1965 introduced a lower classification of pressman (job) for 16 inch up to and including 20 inch which is paid 85 percent of the next wage category. Dennis Molloy, vice-president of the National Association of Union Employers, stated that the introduction of a lower wage rate is the exception and not part of a national trend on the part of the Pressmen's Union to attract noncraft printing by lowering the union wage rate for small press equipment.[30]

The enforcement of the journeyman rule during the last 25 years has shifted unskilled printing production away from unionized plants. The consequences of the journeyman rule has been to limit the union printer's market to products requiring a relatively higher proportion of craft skills and inflate the proportion of commercial printing industry (SIC 275) craftworker employment presented in Table 3.3 above.

Expert opinion indicates that nonunion printers have made the greatest market penetration manufacturing the least complex of printed products. Trieste states that the typographic industry in New York has shifted from union to nonunion production. This has occurred coincident with the expanding capabilities of lower skilled photocomposition to produce more complicated work. Since the early 1970s, nonunion photocomposition plants have displaced union production in all but the most complex advertising and financial typesetting.[31]

The relative complexity of commercial printing production has been established by the Graphic Arts Technical Foundation (GATF) on the basis of surveys. Substitute suppliers, such as in-plant printers, tend to produce short-run, single-color work. Commercial printers, in turn, generally produce larger run, color and, as a rule, more complex work. Competition in the product market is clearly illustrating the ease with which the substitution of unskilled for craft labor can be achieved.[32] Contractual relations, together with the power to strike, cannot isolate union labor from long-range competitive pressures by the new processes.

Proportion of Union Operators

Bloom and Northrup suggest that the long-term success of a union policy regarding technological change hinges upon the economic justification of that policy. Ultimately, the success of a union policy affecting the control of new processes depends upon the relative union/nonunion unit cost of plant output. Without economic justification, nonunion plants or substitute processes and products will continue to erode job opportunities of relatively higher paid union members.

Consistent with this view, Slichter and his co-authors, and Bloom argue that if the work can be done outside shops that the union controls, then the union's effort to compel payment of the journeyman scale will simply force work out of the union shops.[33]

Barnett measures the economic justification of the journeyman rule by comparing the proportion of union to nonunion operators after the introduction of the new equipment. According to Barnett, "A union policy which requires the employment of skilled workmen for work easily within the power of less skilled employees should clearly be uneconomic and its continual enforcement would be against great economic pressure."[34]

Barnett reasons that a trade union policy without economic justification will achieve its chief success at the outset. Thereafter, it will result in a decline in the proportion of union to nonunion operators.[35] Such a decline is seen after the introduction of new process photocomposition, photo-direct offset, and electrostatic equipment.

Since the first shipment of CRT photocomposition equipment in 1967, the proportion of operators in the ITU has declined by more than half. Table 4.3 indicates that in the United States as a whole, union members declined from 70 percent of all Composing Room Workers in the ITU in 1970 to 42 percent in 1980. The decline in the proportion of commercial branch membership in the GCIU is as severe as the membership decline in the ITU. Despite increasing employment opportunities in every represented industry, Table 4.4 indicates that the proportion of operators in the GCIU has declined from 26 percent to only 15 percent in the years 1970 to 1980. In New York City, the displacement of small press work from union plants was so complete that it was unusual to find a single-color press of any description under 29″ in a New York City union shop. Only 20 years earlier, in 1958, equipment in-place surveys indicated that 45 percent of all press equipment performed the same function as and are therefore vulnerable to substitution by duplicating and electrostatic processes.[36]

In contrast to the experience after 1958, Barnett's linotype study is an example of a union policy with economic justification. The enforcement of the journeyman rule during the introduction of the linotype required hand compositors to operate the new machines. In the years following the introduction of the linotype in 1887, the new typesetting equipment was manned by unskilled operators only outside of union plants. Nonunion employers experimented with largely unskilled female operators in this early period. However, the technical character of the linotype required for its most profitable operation both the skills and the level of training of the superseded handcraftsman. The matter set on a linotype is directly proportional to the skill of the operator.[37]

Table 4.3: ITU Commercial Branch Membership as a Proportion of Typesetting Production Employment, 1970 and 1980

Industry of Employment	1970	1980
Commercial Printing (SIC 275)	31,450	18,480
Private Plants	9,000	18,600
Total Employment	41,550	39,280
ITU Membership	29,040	16,335
Proportion of Union Operators	70%	42%

Source: Compiled by the author.

Notes:

1. Table 5.4 is the source of the estimate for private typesetting employment. As seen in this table, private printers had 89 percent of all photocomposition installations in 1978. On the assumption that the average number of production employees in private plants is identical to the average number of production employees in commercial and trade plants, private plant employment is estimated here as 89 percent of commercial (SIC 275) typesetting employment.

2. The membership distribution between the commercial and newspaper branches of the ITU is based upon trade literature. The commercial branch membership distribution for the ITU of 33 percent is taken from *Typographical Journal*, published by the ITU and reported in "Selected Trends of the ITU" (Arlington, VA: Printing Industries of America, Inc., June 2, 1980).

Table 4.4: GCIU Commercial Branch Union Membership as a Proportion of Preparation, Press, and Bindery Production Employment, 1970 and 1980

Industry of Employment	1970	1980
Commercial Printing (SIC 275)	127,860	156,880
Private	358,160	454,960
Quick	2,590	24,494
Total Employment	488,610	636,334
GCIU Membership	125,400	92,700
Proportion of Union Operators	26%	15%

Source: Compiled by the author.

Note: Commercial Branch proportion of union membership is based on expert opinion.

Instead of the strength of the ITU in enforcing the journeyman rule, Barnett attributes the success of this rule to its economic justification. Evidence of economic justification is seen in the stability in the proportion of union operators (94¼ percent and 92 percent, respectively) between 1901 and 1904. Without economic justification, Barnett argues, the journeyman rule would only have achieved its greatest success at the outset.[38]

SUPPORT FOR THE CRAFT RESPONSE MODEL

Trends In Union's Relative Wages and Employment

The union response hypothesis provides an explanation of the significant decline in printing union membership since 1969. Table 4.5 demonstrates that the degree of printing industry unionization declined from 58 percent to 31 percent between 1967 and 1983. The craft union membership model allows for the policy of maximizing either wages or employment within organized plants. Faced with the trade off between wages and employment, economic literature concludes that a high wage rate is a more important union objective than high employment. It is hypothesized that in response to technological displacement of union members during these years, printing unions maintained skilled membership wages. In the case of occupational skill decline, if the union skilled wage is constant relative to those of nonunion, semiskilled workers in general, then it is expected that union employment will decline. The skilled union wage hypothesis is tested by separately comparing union wages with earnings of both manufacturing and printing production workers.

In order to test the hypothesis, two different measures of hourly wages as well as a proxy for nonunion hourly wages are used to estimate union printers' relative earnings in Tables 4.6 and 4.7. The minimum union wage scales provide the numerator of the ratio; average hourly earnings of all manufacturing workers, the denominator. Taken from ITU and GCIU collective bargaining agreements, union hourly wage data are defined as "(1) the basic (minimum) wage rates (excluding holi-

Table 4.5: **Commercial Printing Industry SIC 275 Production Employment, Combined Commercial Branch Membership in the ITU and GCIU, and the Percentage of Printing Industry Unionization, 1967–83.**

Year	Production Employment (1M)	Union Membership (1M)	Unionization (%)
1967	259.5	150.0	58
1969	272.6	154.8	57
1971	268.6	154.1	57
1973	276.0	145.9	53
1975	261.7	136.3	52
1977	272.1	122.1	45
1979	302.5	112.6	37
1981	308.8	108.2	35
1983	318.9	99.2	31

Source: Compiled by the author.

day, vacation or other benefits made regularly or credited to the worker each pay period). . . . Rates over the negotiated minimum which may be paid for special qualifications, or for other reasons, are excluded."[39] While excluded from union wage scales, average hourly earnings of production workers include overtime, premium, and shift differentials.[40] Total industry union and nonunion printing industry (SIC 275) production worker average hourly earnings are used as a proxy for nonunion hourly earnings. Furthermore, union skilled and semiskilled data are a simple average of occupational hourly wage rates within the respective classification "skilled" and "semiskilled." Production worker average hourly earnings, by contrast, are the weighted average of occupational employment and hourly earnings.

As an alternate hypothesis, a concealed increase in the relative skill of union members would also explain the historical rise in relative union wages. However, constant occupational titles, training, and job content of both union skilled and semi-skilled labor remove the possibility of a concealed increase in the relative skill of union membership. Training for all four union craft occupations has remained constant since 1970 (Table 3.1). Job content and training for the three semiskilled union classifications of bindery workers, press assistants, and feeders have remained constant throughout the period 1958–80.

Table 4.6 supports the hypothesis that the ITU and GCIU maintained relative skilled membership wages in response to a decline in the level of printing craftworker skills. Prior to 1968, union craft training remained constant (Table 3.1), while union relative wages and employment increased (Tables 4.5 and 4.6). In contrast, after the reduction in 1969–70 in the values of the printing craftworker skill index, proportional union membership declined in response to the increase in relative union/nonunion skilled wage rates. Compared to all manufacturing production workers, skilled union relative wages increased from 1.40 to 1.62 between 1968 and 1980 (Table 4.6). During a period of increasing printing production employment, Table 4.5 shows that the degree of unionization declined from 58 percent to 22 percent between 1967 and 1983. The relative union wage hypothesis only explains the historical increase in skilled union wages and does not consider the increase in semi-skilled union wage rates.

While Table 4.7 is consistent with the relative wage hypothesis, the measure of union wages relative to those of printing production workers is less useful because of the high level and significant change in the degree of unionization of printing industry production workers. The significant decline in the proportion of union printing production employment (Table 4.5) explains at least part of the rise in union skilled and semiskilled wages relative to all printing production workers. The ratio's denominator, printing production average hourly earnings,

Table 4.6: Ratio of Skilled and Semiskilled Union Printing Production Average Minimum Hourly Wage Rate to Average Hourly Earnings of all Manufacturing Production Workers, 1958–80.

Year	Skilled	Semiskilled
1958	1.49	1.17
1963	1.49	1.18
1967	1.53	1.16
1973	1.65	1.27
1978	1.58	1.26
1980	1.62	1.31

Source: Compiled by the author.
Notes:
1. Printing trade occupational wage rates published periodically in *Union Wages and Hours: Printing Industry* are divided into skilled workers and into a second grouping combining semiskilled workers. Skilled workers are defined to be those journeymen, typesetters, preparation and press workers, or bookbinders who completed respective apprenticeship programs. Skilled workers have the journeymen titles of Bookbinders, Compositors, Machine Operators, (Linotype) Machinists and Cylinder Pressmen. Semiskilled and unskilled workers include occupational titles of Binderywomen (Bookbinders II) and Press Assistants and Feeders. When first published, five lithography occupational wage rates are added in 1967. Skilled lithography workers are journeymen, cameramen, platemakers, pressmen (offset), and strippers.
2. Semiskilled workers are defined to be press assistants and feeders.

Table 4.7: Ratio of Skilled and Semiskilled Printing Union Average Minimum Hourly Wage Rate to Average Hourly Earnings of Commercial Printing Industry SIC 275 Production Workers, 1958–80.

Year	Skilled	Semiskilled
1958	1.27	0.87
1963	1.26	0.89
1967	1.32	0.94
1973	1.40	1.08
1978	1.45	1.16
1980	1.49	1.22

Source: Compiled by the author.
Note: See notes 1 and 2, Table 4.6.

includes both union and nonunion employment. Since skilled union wages are significantly greater than the average of printing production workers, then a significant decline in the number of skilled union members employed in the printing industry would, in itself, increase the relative union wage rate.

CURRENT EXPLANATIONS OF
UNION MEMBERSHIP DECLINE

A General Theory of Labor Market Transformation

Gordon, Edwards, and Reich argue that technological change is exploited by employers in a conscious effort to control labor. Rather than serving as an independent determinant, technology serves as an instrument useful for not only improving profits but for controlling the shop floor as well. In *Segmented Work, Divided Workers,* the authors state that after World War II technology tended to extend a qualitatively greater degree of control over the activities of production. They state, "Where it emerged, it reduced the degree of independent leverage that workers could maintain over the pace and quality of their work.... The new technology substantially reduced the independence in production of workers in the skilled trades."[41]

Hence, rather than being technically determined, *Segmented Work, Divided Workers* argues that the organization of work in the printing industry is transformed by people and class. In this model, production workers are not merely passive pawns but, through worker and union effort, are able to play an instrumental role in shaping the structure of the capitalist economy. Specifically, the printers and their unions might redress the shift in power to management that was induced by the technological reorganization of production during the 1958–83 period.[42]

In another work, *Contested Terrain,* Edwards expands the argument that the "social" element is an important dimension in the choice of production technology. In addition to technical efficiency and the costs of inputs/values of outputs, Edwards sees the third factor entering into the calculation of profitability as the leverage that the new processes provide management in transforming purchased labor power into labor actually performed. He argues that the conscious design of capital in controlling labor is critical to the choice of technology. Accordingly, Edwards states:

> Mechanization often brings with it technical control as the worker loses control of the pace and sequence of tasks, but this consequence must nearly always be understood as the result of the *particular* capitalist design of technology and not an inherent characteristic of machinery in *general.*[43]

In this context, the historical transformation of labor in the United States is seen as divided into three stages. The processes of homogenization and segmentation provide an understanding of the recent transformation of union power in the printing industry. The initial proletarianization of labor began in the 1820s and continued throughout the remainder of the nineteenth century. The characteristic development of this wage-labor system took place in a country relatively free from feudal traditions and with a large supply of fertile land available for agriculture. In *Segmented Work,* we read,

> Throughout the period of rapid growth from the 1850s through the early 1870s, several relatively diverse internal systems of "labor control" in production co-existed corresponding at least in part to the respective characteristics of the sources of labor supply. As a result, the labor market continued to be divided into distinct pockets; a single, generalized, homogenous and universally competitive arena for the exchange of labor power did not yet exist.[44]

While the process of homogenization in the U. S. economy became increasingly more dominant after the 1920s, the evolution of the workplace is similar to the deskilling process experienced by printers after 1958. Employers responded to their problems in labor productivity in the late nineteenth century with mechanization, greater use of foremen to supervise workers, and a decreasing reliance on skilled labor. Again, we read in Gordon, Edwards, and Reich:

> The early effects of the homogenization period included increasing capital-labor ratios and plant size transformed labor process with an increase in the proportion of operatives, a slight decrease in skill differential, the spread of a national labor market, and most important, a vastly expanded effective labor supply.[45]

And, in a description similar to the experience of printers in the last 20 years, they state:

> More and more jobs in the capitalist sector of the economy were reduced to a common semiskilled operative denominator and control of the labor process became concentrated among employers and their foremen, who used direct supervision or machine pacing to "drive" their workers. The labor market became increasingly generalized and much more competitive. Skills were much less controlled by the workers.[46]

One of the most significant influences of technology upon union power has been the shift in the mechanism for transmitting new skills from printers to the control of employers. Gordon describes this initial proletarianization phase during which skilled workers controlled the labor process.

In the initial proletarianization phase, skilled workers controlled the labor process. They hired apprentices or helpers who gained skills while working alongside the artisan or master. The transmission of skills from one cohort to another thus passed through the bottleneck of the skilled workers, who could regulate the terms and magnitude of the transmission process. Indeed, this bottleneck (and the control that skilled workers exercised over the level of output) constituted one of the main incentives for capitalists to enter the workplace and transform the labor process.[47]

The demise of the apprenticeship system created a vacuum that is presently being filled by a combination of industry vocational schools, formal college training, and a limited number of apprenticeship programs no longer solely controlled by skilled workers.

The segmentation process began in the 1920s and, as stated, was characterized by the corporate exploitations of new mechanisms for more effective and reliable labor control.

Although the so-called drive system did not disappear, it was replaced in many sectors by services of structured rules and incentives including, but not limited to, collective bargaining agreements. General skills were increasingly transmitted through the educational system.[48]

In their joint work, Gordon, Edwards and Reich argue that the reason for the decline of union power is the internal divisions of working classes along many economic, political, and cultural lines. The source of working-class cleavages is the structural and qualitative differences in jobs and labor markets through which workers secure their livelihood. The segmentation of labor in the printing industry is rooted in craft unionism. As Gordon and his co-authors suggest, craft unions concentrated on consolidating and protecting members' gains in an industry where they had already established influence.[49] Subsequently, as the deskilling process continued, printing unions represented an increasingly smaller proportion of the labor supply.

Gordon, Edwards, and Reich suggest that, in addition to craft union inertia, the decline in union membership is a consequence of new production processes developed by printing management in order to achieve more effective control the workforce. Specifically, employers consciously develop new processes that increase the labor supply by permitting management to substitute lesser skilled workers for craft labor. While the argument of these authors might possibly explain the decline in unionization, a more detailed analysis of the commercial printing industry suggests that management behavior is not a necessary determinant of the decline in union membership.[50]

Indeed, Gordon, Edwards, and Reich themselves suggest that their argument might not be applicable to the printing industry because plants are characteristically small and immobile within a competitive market. In contrast to the "core" firms as defined in *Segmented Work,* the 25,841 commercial printing plants surveyed only employed an average of 13 office and production workers each in 1977. Also analogous to the experience of the mining industry in the early 1900s, printing plants are unable to flee to "industrial satellite suburbs" because their markets are local.[51]

The drive to reduce unit cost is the primary basis of process selection, not development, in the commercial printing industry. Competitive pressures mandate that production techniques be chosen on the basis of relative unit cost since printers supply a product with a high degree of substitution between products, processes, and suppliers. The market in which the printing capitalist operates is independent of his influence and, consequently, may impose on this employer motivations separate from any desire for greater control of the labor process.

Printing firms purchase new technology because they are too small to develop their own production processes. Printing plants are service organizations limited to providing custom orders to local markets with techniques that are commonly available. Commercial, as well as in-plant and quick printers, are consumers of new process equipment. In contrast to large innovative firms such as Polaroid, printers are technological followers in applying new techniques to production. As we have seen in Chapter 2, employers adopted technologies developed outside of the commercial printing industry. Specifically, the three major skill-reducing innovations—CRT photocomposition, photo-direct offset, and electrophotography—were developed by a wide range of equipment manufacturers. Minor preparation and press innovations, for example, were developed by such nonprinting firms as Eastman-Kodak and the Harris Corporation.

Rather than printing management, the driving force of new printing technology is the manufacturers of capital goods. It is the motivation of equipment manufacturers, not printing management, that explains the development of new production technologies. Equipment manufacturers are not limited to local markets. They are able to reduce unit costs by expanding their unit sales in international markets. In order to expand their market for printing equipment, capital goods manufacturers have simplified the typesetting and printing processes. By requiring only semi- or unskilled labor, equipment manufacturers have expanded their market share from the traditional printing plant to any commercial, industrial, or service establishment. The equipment manufacturers' market is no longer limited by industry-specific craft skills.

Still another view holds that management resistance, in the form of changes in corporate structure and the outmigration of firms from traditional printing centers, independently contributes to the transformation of the industry labor market. Specifically, this view states that since the early 1960s three main factors have combined to create changes in labor market unionization.

> New technology, rapidly introduced, not only greatly increased productivity but also reduced printers' control over the work process. Secondly, a great number of firms were reorganized through mergers and acquisitions thereby creating many multiple plant operations. Finally, the industry witnessed a strong outmigration of firms from traditional printing centers.[52]

The effect of these factors will now be evaluated.

Multiple Plant Operations and Outmigration as Agents of Change

This view holds that through the processes of merger and acquisition the industry was reorganized into more powerful firms in both newspaper and commercial printing production. In 1967, for example, Giebel shows that there were 24 separate mergers within the newspaper segment of the industry, and that these reorganizations involved more than 6 percent of the entire newspaper employment. On this basis, and on the basis of what limited Department of Commerce data are available on commercial printers, Giebel concludes that multiple plant firms had a devastating influence on the labor market. Also included as a basis in Giebel's conclusion is the fact that eight chains greatly expanded the number of plants they controlled during the 1960s and early 1970s.[53]

Since 1954, the classification "multi-unit company" depends on whether or not a company operates at more than one location within the time span of each census. Any company with one manufacturing plant and a nonmanufacturing or administrative office unit located elsewhere is by these criteria termed a multi-unit company.

A second variant of the multiple plant hypothesis is that unionized printers, by establishing a second nonunion plant, are a cause of declining industry unionization. This hypothesis is also suggested by industry experts Gill and Sommer. In 1973, Donald Sommer, executive vice-president of the Master Printers of America, stated in an internal memorandum to the nonunion membership: "One reason for the decline in union membership is the opening of branch plants away from the home office by large unionized printing establishments. These plants operate as open shops.[54]

Prior to the 1971 decline in printing union membership, there is evidence that the percent of industry employment in multiple plant firms increased from 31 to 40 percent between 1957 and 1967. However, contrary to the multiple plant hypothesis, after 1967 multiple plant employment declined significantly to 34 percent in 1982 as indicated in Table 4.8.

Moreover there is no evidence of a significant increase in the influence of conglomerate chain operatives as asserted by Giebel. The small number and the separate industry classifications of the acquiring companies suggest that mergers and acquisitions are not significant factors in the restructuring of the labor market. Department of Commerce data indicate that the total number of commercial printing acquisitions reached 20 in 1967. This was twice as many as in 1966. Of the 65 acquisitions of commercial printers in the five-year period between 1963 and 1967, only 10 percent were horizontal. Most of the acquiring companies were not even classified by the Department of Commerce as printing and publishing concerns.[55]

Later, in 1973–74, there were 13 combined commercial printing and manifold business forms establishments with over 500 employees acquired by 12 companies. Seven acquiring companies were not in the printing and publishing industry.[56]

The commercial printing industry (SIC 275) data available indicate no discernable pattern of concentration during the period 1963–72 or in 1977. According to Lofquist, letterpress commercial printing concentra-

Table 4.8   Employment Trends in SIC 275, Commercial Printing Multiple Plant Firms, 1954–82 *(in thousands of production workers)*

Year	Multiple Plant Employment	Total Industry Employment	Multiple Plant/ Total Industry(%)
1954	85.7	278.0	31
1958	97.0	278.7	35
1963	106.9	291.3	37
1967	128.7	321.6	40
1972	122.8	314.5	39
1977	127.5	327.2	39
1982	140.7	415.5	34

Source: Compiled by the author.
Notes:
1. SIC 275 data were collected by combining SIC 2751 (commercial printing, letterpress) and SIC 2752 (commercial printing, lithographic).
2. Production employment data, unfortunately, are available only in 1967, 1972, 1977, and 1982.

tion of the 50 largest companies decreased from 38 to 31 percent of industry shipments during this time. The percent value of these shipments accounted for by groupings of the largest 4, 8, and 20 companies in either letterpress or lithography did not increase more than 1 percent in any category during this same time period.[57]

Geographic Dispersion and Unionization

In 1979, Gregory Giebel argued that a strong outward migration of firms from traditional printing centers was a third factor, together with technological change and corporate reorganization, serving to transform the industry's labor market structure. Giebel's theory is not uncommon and is, in fact, suggested by Nelson R. Eldred. While Giebel never defines "outmigration," Eldred specified that plants migrate to either the sunbelt or the suburbs.[58] This section, therefore, will consider the relation between geographic dispersion and union structure. The argument that plant migration to these areas significantly influenced printing center unionization will also be considered.

The geographic structure of the printing industry is conditioned by proximity to the consumer and the location of particular resources. The primary determinant of the geographical dispersion of commercial printing is market demand. Since commercial printing is consumed by other industries for communications, packaging, and resale, printing production mirrors the dispersion of manufacturing and service sectors of the economy as a whole.[59]

The basic unit of printing industry union structure is the local craft union. The three major crafts organized these national unions during the last half of the nineteenth century. Local chapters, for example, established the National Typographical Union in 1852. The Men's International Printing Press Union of North America was organized in 1889. Finally, in 1892, the bookbinders seceded from the ITU and began the International Brotherhood of Bookbinders.[60]

Table 4.9 indicates that the number of ITU locals declined from 845 in 1947 to 591 in 1978. Combined GCIU locals were reduced from 1,113 to 857 during this same period.

Local craft union jurisdiction is limited to a specific geographic area and mirrors the decentralized printing industry product market. This area usually coincides with the political boundaries of a city or county. The strength of the local depends upon the concentration of printing production. Historically, the largest concentration of both union membership and printing production is found in New York, Chicago, Los Angeles, and Philadelphia.[61]

Table 4.9   Distribution of National Unions, 1947-78 *(by number of locals)*

Union	1947	1957	1978
International Typographical Union (ITU)	856	785	591
Printing and Graphic Communications Union, International (IPGCU)[1]			635
Printing Pressmen[1]	606	750	(note 4)
Stereotypers[1]	172	179	(note 4)
Graphic Arts International Union (GAIU)[1]			222
Photo-engravers[1]	90	101	(note 2)
Bookbinders[1]	245	220	(note 3)

Source: Compiled by the author.
Notes:
1.   By July 1, 1983 these unions had merged into the GCUI.
2.   Merged into Lithographers and Photoengravers International Union, September 7, 1964.
3.   Merged into Graphic Arts International Union, September 4, 1972.
4.   Merged to form the Printing and Graphic Communications Union, International, October 17, 1973.
5.   American Lithographers Association (ALA) was disaffiliated with the AFL–CIO on August 21, 1958 and membership data are not included in this table.

The size of a local's membership usually determines its financial resources and strength. If the local is small, then it generally cannot afford full-time officials. Large locals have been almost semi-autonomous bodies. Small locals, however, rely heavily on the international union. With little interference from the international, large locals often carry out their own collective bargaining and grievance procedures and even resolve their own internal disputes.[62]

The purpose of plant relocation is the reduction of production costs. Labor cost reduction is particularly important. In fact, Giebel clearly states that a reduction in labor costs is the primary cause of plant relocations away from traditional printing centers and their relatively expensive collective bargaining agreements. Loft confirms Giebel's view by stating that there is a direct relation between the migration of commercial printing and geographic variation in production costs. Specifically, he concludes that the variation in union wages of commercial printing is the most significant factor in determining production location.[63]

Gustafson's analysis of the cost of printing production in New York furthers this view. He states that because of the geographic uniformity in paper prices—the most important of all material costs—the cost of materials can be eliminated in relocational considerations. Gustafson also argues that labor is the largest cost component and, therefore, is the

Table 4.10   City and Population Variation in Union Printing Trades, 1958 and 1980 *(average hourly rate)*

Membership Populations	1958	1980
All Commercial Printing Union Members	2.85	10.29
Average for Population Group		
Group I (1,000,000 or more)	3.07	11.48
Group II (500,000 to 1,000,000)	2.74	9.83
Group III (250,000 to 500,000)	2.78	9.53
Group IV (100,000 to 250,000)	2.62	9.22

Source: Compiled by the author.
Note: The last issue of *Union Wages and Benefits: Printing Trades* was published for the year 1982.

dominant force affecting printing production location choices. Using the *Census of Manufacturers* for 1954 as a source, he shows that production payroll comprises almost 50 percent of commercial printing value added. His case study of New York City manufacturing concludes: "The principal reason for the migration of printing from the New York City metropolitan region is the region's top labor cost position."[64]

Table 4.10 shows the direct variation between the average hourly wage rate, concentration of market, and size of population. In both 1958 and 1978, union wages in the top five printing centers comprising *Population Group I* (Chicago, Detroit, Los Angeles, New York, and Philadelphia) exceeded the national hourly averages for union wages. San Francisco was the only other printing center to exceed the national average in both 1958 and 1978. Giebel quotes Lipset but relies on the generally accepted assumption that the individual craft locals in New York, Chicago, Los Angeles, and Philadelphia are relatively strong and traditionally expect the largest industry settlements for their members.

Unfortunately, it is not possible to independently obtain data verifying this apparent relationship between local union size and wage settlements. Lipset, however, confirms the direct relation between local union size and wages, after conducting a case study of New York ITU Local No. 6.[65] Separately Munson established the concentration of National Amalgamated Lithographers of America (ALA) membership in large metropolitan areas. According to Munson, half of the ALA membership is concentrated within the New York, Chicago, and San Francisco metropolitan areas during the years between 1957 and 1961. These membership data are summarized in Table 4.11.

Assuming that the degree of unionization in metropolitan areas is higher than that in nonmetropolitan areas, Giebel undertakes an examination of production concentration in the largest 10 and 50 printing centers throughout the 1950s and in 1963. It should be noted that

Table 4.11   Amalgamated Lithographers of America (ALA) Union Membership, 1957–60

Year	Total Members	Local 1 New York	Local 2 Chicago	Local 17 San Francisco	Total Number of Locals
1957	34,133	7,558	4,730	2,151	85
1958	35,087	7,627	4,853	2,145	89
1959	35,996	7,699	4,919	2,161	93
1960	37,959	8,058	5,053	2,218	95

Source: Munson, Fred C., *Labor Relations in the Lithographic Industry,* appendix C. Cambridge, MA: Harvard University Press, 1963, 244–5.

Giebel uses no data published after his reference to the "Quarterly Industry Reports" appearing in 1972 *Printing and Publishing* in support of his hypothesis. Giebel's hypothesis appeared in the Winter of 1979.[66]

Census data indicate that printing employment is highly concentrated in the 20 largest metropolitan printing centers. Data for comparable Standard Metropolitan Statistical Areas (SMSA) gathered from 1968 through 1978 indicate that nearly half of industry employment is concentrated therein. While growing slower than the entire industry rate, employment in the largest printing centers declined from 54 percent of total industry employment in 1968 to only 47 percent in 1978. These data are summarized in Table 4.12. The number of printing centers is limited to 20 since, in either 1968 or 1978, the smallest printing SMSA contributed a maximum of 1 percent of concentrated employment. Giebel also considered the top ten printing centers in 1963. A printing center SMSA is defined as a single economic and social community with a large volume of daily travel and communication between central city (having a population of 50,000 or more) and outlying parts of the area. Each area consists of one or more whole counties.[67]

Statistical data show, however, that coinciding with the general migration of industry to the south and west, there has been a redistribution of printing plants from the east and central states to the sunbelt. While total employment increased a nominal 6 percent in 20 centers, the five sunbelt SMSAs increased from 29,016 in 1968 to 40,748 in 1978. This represents an increase of 40 percent. The sunbelt is that part of the United States below the southern boundaries of Virginia, Kentucky, Missouri, Kansas, Colorado, and Utah and then across to the Pacific Coast.[68]

However, there is no evidence to support Giebel's hypothesis that plant outmigration from major printing centers is a major cause of union membership decline. If the data were available, Giebel's hypothesis could be tested by comparing metropolitan SMSA and national

Table 4.12:   Twenty Largest Metropolitan Commercial Printing Centers, SIC 275, 1968 and 1978 (plants and total employment)

Metropolitan Printing SMSAs	1968		1978	
	Plants	Employment	Plants	Employment
Commercial Printing Total	17,579	333,590	21,421	397,620
Twenty Metropolitan Centers Total	8,407	176,451	9,334	187,637
Individual Totals for the Twenty Centers				
Atlanta	120	3,857	249	5,913
Boston	446	9,121	494	10,388
Chicago	1,086	36,233	1,142	32,178
Cincinnati	160	5,703	771	5,427
Cleveland	262	4,074	299	5,315
Dallas—Ft. Worth*	276	4,519	404	6,497
Detroit	361	6,730	341	6,102
Houston*	149	2,532	235	3,997
Los-Angeles— Long Beach	964	13,453	1,087	20,287
Miami*	152	2,037	226	2,705
Milwaukee	157	6,049	209	6,578
Minneapolis— St. Paul	209	7,086	284	8,088
Nassau—Suffolk	202	3,592	356	5,501
Newark	248	3,666	279	4,877
New York	2,131	33,545	1,788	27,354
Philadelphia	497	15,043	578	13,019
Pittsburgh	163	2,811	176	3,193
St. Louis	251	5,174	274	5,281
San Francisco— Oakland*	361	6,475	450	7,260
Washington, DC	212	4,751	292	6,582

Source: **U.S. Department of Commerce. "Major Centers of Commercial Printing," by Charles R. Cook.** *Printing and Publishing Quarterly,* **(Fall 1981): 15–17.**
   * **indicates a sunbelt SMSA**

ratios of union membership as a percentage of industry employment. Giebel's hypothesis would be supported if the unionization of SMSAs declined faster than the national printing industry ratio of membership to production employment.

The metropolitan concentration of printing production employment did not significantly diminish when compared with an 112,000 decline in paid union membership between 1969 and 1983. Table 4.12

indicates that total employment in the largest metropolitan centers actually increased by 11,186 between 1960 and 1978. Craft membership depends primarily upon production employment, and the use of available total employment data assumes a constant ratio of production to total employment. Data published in *Employment and Earnings* indicate that the national ratio of production employment to total employment declined from 78 percent in 1968 to 74 percent in 1978. The 4 percent decline explains the decrease of 25,170 in national production employment in 1978. By offsetting the 11,186 increase in total employment against the decrease in the proportion of production employment, or 15,170, we can see that production employment in the 20 centers declined by approximately 4,000 between 1968 and 1978.[69]

Only four SMSAs, New York, Chicago, Philadelphia and Detroit, actually decreased in total employment. Combined total employment declined by 12,600, or 6 percent, when compared with the employment figures for 1968 for the 20 largest centers. This, too, is seen in Table 4.12.

Table 4.13 suggests that printing plants tend to relocate away from central urban areas rather than move large distances from their product market. Since urban commercial printing employment data are not available, this study measures the dispersion from urban areas by comparing county and SMSA production employment data between 1967 and 1982. This is done, however, only in the four SMSAs that actually experienced a decrease in production employment. It is important to note that in each case where comparative data are available, the central county of each metropolitan area experienced a greater decrease in production employment than outlying areas.

There is no evidence to suggest that these plant relocations outside central urban areas displace union membership. It is customary, for instance, for relocating plants in the area of New York City to either employ union labor from the new location or transfer previous union labor with the plant. Outside the central city location, plants realize a lower union wage and occupancy costs.[70] Previous case studies confirm that plants relocate production within a particular local market area but outside the jurisdictional boundaries of high wage craft union locals. Giebel states that improved forms of transportation allow printers to supply local markets outside of the perimeter of the higher paid metropolitan locals. Case studies by Gustafson, Drake, and Seybold also indicate that union plants relocate to adjacent suburbs in order to reduce labor and occupancy costs while maintaining access to the product market.

Sommer states that the conversion of union to nonunion plants is a second cause of union membership decline. He states,

Table 4.13: Commercial Printing SIC 275 County and SMSA Employment Decline in Chicago, Detroit, Philadelphia, New York, 1967, 1977 and 1982 *(production workers)*

	1967	1977	1982	Employment Decline 1967–82
Chicago				
Cook County	27,500	20,300	19,400	8,100
SMSA	NA	24,400	24,200	NA
Detroit				
Wayne County	4,500	3,000	2,500	2,000
SMSA	5,100	4,200	3,900	1,200
Phildelphia				
Philadelphia County	7,300	5,100	NA	NA
SMSA	9,500	9,500	9,600	300
New York				
New York County	19,200	12,600	13,300	5,900
SMSA	30,300	25,900	26,700	3,600

Source: Compiled by the author.
Notes:
1. Chicago Standard Metropolitan Statistical Area (SMSA) includes the Counties of Cook, DuPage, Kane, Lake, McHenry, and Will Counties between 1967 and 1977.
2. In 1967 the Detroit SMSA included the counties of Macomb, Oakland and Wayne. In 1977 the additional counties of Lapeer, Livingston, and Saint Clair are included and has the effect of decreasing relative SMSA employment decline.
3. Philadelphia, Pa.-New Jersey SMSA consist of Bucks, Chester, Delaware, Montgomery, and Philadelphia Counties, Pa., and Burlington, Camden, and Gloucester Counties, N.J.

> There is another trend for unionized establishments to "go open,"
> either by decertification process; or by the employees voting to
> throw the union out; or via the employer withdrawing from the bar-
> gaining unit, bargaining to an impasse, and then replacing the
> struck workers who were union members.[71]

However, sufficient data are not available to indicate the frequency of success of employers converting union plants into nonunion plants. The National Labor Relations Board (NLRB) publishes the number of representation cases annually, but does so only for the aggregate industry classification of printing, publishing, and allied industry. The relative employment of the two industry classifications indicates the inappropriateness of the more aggregate data. In 1981, for example, printing and publishing (SIC 27) employed 699,300 while commercial printing (SIC 275) employed less than half of that number of production workers (308,800). Only 64 of the total 279 petitions for the determination of collective bargaining representation filed in 1981 were not initiated by labor organizations. The 59 petitions filed by employees and 15 representation cases filed by employers to determine representation might be considered at an extreme as an index of printing and publishing management resistance to unionization. In addition, the NLRB reports that in 1981 only seven petitions were filed in the entire printing and publishing industry requesting an election to determine whether or not the union's authority to enter into a union shop contract should be rescinded. While suggested by the aggregate printing and publishing data from the NLRB, the infrequency of commercial printing plant decertification between 1969 and 1981 is confirmed by national union employer negotiator Dennis Molloy.[72]

Indeed, the lack of an increase in printing management resistance to unionization is indicated by the relatively few "defense kits" that the nonunion employers' association distributes to a member who is threatened by a union organization drive. The national nonunion printing employers association reports that between 1967 and 1983 an annual maximum of 58 master printers "defense kits" were distributed. Between 1979 and 1984, the Master Printers mailed 30, 58, 52, 17, 25, and 38 defense kits, respectively.[73]

SUMMARY

The ITU and GCIU are shown to have maintained membership wages in the wake of printing production skill decline. In the case of partial skill displacement, it is indicated that skilled union/nonunion wage rates increased after the decline of the printing craft worker skill index. In the case of complete craft skill displacement, the relative union wage rate has been maintained at significantly higher rates for the operation of new process equipment. The decline in the total, as well as the separate typesetting and printing sector proportions of union operators since 1967 is indicative of the influence of work rule policies upon union membership.

Corporate restructuring, as an alternative explanation, ignores industry acquisition and multiple plant employment data. Local product market structure prevents the outmigration of plants to the sunbelt, and collective bargaining agreements eliminate the possibility of moving an existing union plant to a suburban location without continuation of contract provisions. Instead of double breasting and management conversion of union to open shops, there is increased substitution in the product market between union and nonunion printing suppliers. However, while the data presented does not support the management resistance hypothesis, it also does not disprove this competing explanation. Without more complete data to quantify trends in management resistance to union formation, industry specific NLRB election data and union organizing expenditures, for example, the alternate explanation cannot be rejected.

NOTES

1. Harold V. Semling, Jr., "Trade Unions Eye Merger Route as Path to National Unity," *Printing Management*, February 1974, 33 (hereafter cited as "Eye Merger Route").

2. "North America's Largest Graphic Arts Union Created in Vote Avalanche by 81% of GAUI and 78% of IPCGU," *Union Tabloid*, 30 June 1983, 1 (hereafter cited as "Vote Avalanche").

3. "President's Talk Details ITU Goal," *International Typographical Union Review*, 24(16):1 (hereafter cited as "President's Talk"); and Bingel, "Be Proud of Union," *International Typographical Union Review*, Conv. Is., 1981, 1 (hereafter cited as "Proud of Union").

4. Kenneth J. Brown and Alexander J. Rohan, "Union Labor 1973," *Inland Printer/American Lithographer*, 170(5):42 (hereafter cited as "Union Labor").

5. Thomas B. Cosden, "Management May Be Up Against A Strong Bargaining Power," *Printing Management*, July 1971, 130.

6. Semling, "Eye Merger Route," 33.

7. Barnett, *Chapters*, 123.

8. Robert Wallis, "Automation and Restrictive Labor Agreement," *Printing World*, 188(16):394.

9. "Contract for Book and Job Work Between Printers' League Section, Printing Industries of Metropolitan New York, Inc., and New York Typographical Union No. 6," for period 1967-70, 89.

10. U. S. Department of Commerce. Bureau of the Census. "Transportation Patterns of Printed and Published Products," table 6 prepared by Dorothy B. Hokkanen, *Printing and Publishing*, (October 1970):10.

11. Semling, "Eye Merger Route," 32-4.

12. Semling, "Eye Merger Route," 33.

13. "Vote Avalanche," *Union Tabloid*, 1.

14. Semling, "Eye Merger Route," 33; "Vote Avalanche," *Union Tabloid*, 1, and "Bit of GCIU History," *Graphics Communication International Union Newspaper*, July 1981, 8.

15. Bloom and Northrup, *Labor Relations*, 12.

16. U. S. Department of Labor. Bureau of Labor Statistics. *Employment and Earnings*, 116; and U. S. Department of Labor. Bureau of Labor Statistics. *Employment and Earnings*, supplement dated July 1983, 185.

17. "Proud of Union," *International Typographical Union Review*, 1.

18. Semling, "Eye Merger Route," 35.

19. U. S. Department of Labor. Bureau of Labor Statistics. "Appendix I: Membership by Industry Group," *Directory of National Union and Employee Association* (Washington, DC: GPO, 1980), 105-7.

20. GATF, *Niche 1,* 1.

21. James E. Horne. Interview with the author, 11 April 1983 (hereafter cited as Horne, 4/83). Horne was the employer negotiator for this association; and Dennis Molloy. Telephone conversation with the author, 6 May 1983 (hereafter cited as Molloy, 5/83).

22. "Contract for Book and Job Work Between Printers' League Section, Printing Industries of Metropolitan New York, Inc. and New York Typographical Union No. 6." 1975, 5 (hereafter cited as: "Metropolitan, 1975").

23. "Contract for Book and Job Work Between Printers' League Section, Printing Industries of Metropolitan New York, Inc. and New York Typographical Union No. 6," for period 1955–57; 5-6 (hereafter cited as "Metropolitan, 1955–57").

24. Ibid., 6-7.

25. "Contract for Book and Job Work Between Printers' League Section, Printing Industries of Metropolitan New York, Inc. and New York Typographical Union No. 6," for the period 1975–83, 105–6 (hereafter cited as "Metropolitan, 1975–83"); and "Contract for Book and Job Work Between Printers' League Section, Printing Industries of Metropolitan New York, Inc. and New York Typographical Union No. 6," for the period 1983–89 (hereafter cited as "Metropolitan, 1983–89").

26. James E. Horne. Interview with the author, New York, New York, 1 March 1984 (hereafter cited as Horne, 3/84); "Contract for Book and Job Work Between Printers' League Section, Printing Industries of Metropolitan New York, Inc. and New York Printing Pressmen's Union, No. 1," for the period 1957–59, Part IX: "Character of Work," 44; "Contract for Book and Job Work Between Printers' League Section, Printing Industries of Metropolitan New York, Inc. and New York Printing Pressmen's Union, No. 51," for the period 1957–59, Part X: "Complement of Men," 44–6; "Contract for Book and Job Work Between Printers' League Section, Printing Industries of Metropolitan New York, Inc. and New York Printing Pressmen's Union, No. 51," for the period 1981–83, Part XIII: "Character of Work," 64; and "Contract for Book and Job Work Between Printers' League Section, Printing Industries of Metropolitan New York, Inc. and New York Printing Pressmen's Union, No. 51," for the period 1981–83, Part XIV: "Complement of Men," 64–8.

27. "Contract for Book and Job Work Between Printers' League Section, Printing Industries of Metropolitan New York, Inc. and New York Papercutters and Bookbinders Union, No. 119B–43B," for the period 1956–58, Part X: "Complement of Men," 18; and "Contract for Book and Job Work Between Printers' League Section, Printing Industries of Metropolitan New York, Inc. and New York Papercutters and Bookbinders Union, No. 119B–43B," for the period 1984–86; Part X: "Complement of Equipment," 44–5.

28. Master Printers' Section. Printing Industries of Metropolitan New York, Inc. "1977 Recommended Standards of Minimum Wages, Hours and Benefits." Approved at a Special Meeting for the period 1 January 1977 to 31 December 1977, 1; and U. S. Department of Labor. Bureau of Labor Statistics. *Metropolitan Areas, United States and Regional Summaries,* bulletin 1950-77 (Washington, DC: GPO, 1980), 49.

29. While the Contract for Local No. 6 of the ITU dated 4 October 1975 established a new semiskilled classification entitled "Computer Typist," a wage scale has yet to be determined; "Metropolitan, 1975–1983," 127; and U. S. Department of Labor. Bureau of Labor Statistics. *Metropolitan Areas,* 49.

30. "Contract for Book and Job Offices between Printers' League Section, Printing Industries of Metropolitan New York, Inc., and New York Printing Pressmen's Union No. 51," for period 1962–64, 20, (hereafter cited as "Metropolitan, 1962–1964"); "Contract for Book and Job Offices between Printers' League Section, Printing Industries of Metropolitan New York, Inc., and New York Printing Pressmen's Union No. 51," for the period

1964–66, 28, (hereafter cited as "Metropolitan, 1964–66"); James E. Horne. Interview with the author, 7 April 1983, hereafter cited as Horne. 4/83; and J. Dennis Molloy. Telephone interview with the author, 2 July 1985 (hereafter cited as "Molloy, 7/85").

31.   Trieste, 8/24.

32.   Mulvey, *Trade Unions*, 63.

33.   Bloom and Northrup, *Economics of Labor*, 252–3; Slichter, et al., Impact, 364–5; and Lloyd Ulman, *The Rise of the National Trade Unions* (Cambridge, MA: Harvard University Press, 1962), 306 (hereafter cited as *National Unions).*

34.   Barnett, *Chapter,* 27.

35.   Ibid., 28.

36.   James E. Horne. Interview with the author, New York, New York, 28 June 1983 (hereafter cited as Horne, 6/28); and U. S. Department of Commerce. Business and Defense Services Administration. "Letterpress and Lithographic Printing Presses in Place in the United States by State and Region," Quarterly Industry Report prepared by Charles R. Cook and Theodore C. Collins, *Printing and Publishing* (July 1964):7-10.

37.   Barnett, *Chapters,* 28–9.

38.   Barnett, *Chapters,* 26, 28, 29.

39.   U. S. Department of Labor, Bureau of Labor Statistics. *Union Wages and Hours: Printing Industry,* September 2, 1980, bulletin 2125, p. 2.

40.   U. S. Department of Labor, Bureau of Labor Statistics. *Employment and Earnings in the United States,* 1909–78, bulletin 1312-11 (Washington: GPO, 1979), 943.

41.   David M. Gordon, Richard Edwards, and Michael Reich, *Segmented Work, Divided Workers* (Cambridge, MA: Harvard University Press, 1982, 186–7 (hereafter cited as *Segmented Work).* Reprinted with permission of publisher.

42.   Ibid., 17, 41.

43.   Richard Edwards, *Contested Terrain* (New York: Basic Books, 1979), 112 (hereafter cited as *Terrain).*

44.   Gordon, et al., *Segmented Work,* 14.

45.   Ibid., 14.

46.   Ibid., 3.

47.   Ibid., 247.

48.   Ibid., 3.

49.   Ibid., 159.

50.   Ibid., 161.

51.   U. S. Department of Commerce. Bureau of the Census. *1977 Census of Manufacturers,* Table 4: "Commercial and Manifold Business Forms" (Washington, DC: GPO, 1980), 18; Cook, "Presses in Place," 3; and Gordon, et al., *Segmented Work,* 158–9.

52.   Gregory Giebel, "Corporate Structure, Technology and the Printing Industry," *Labor Studies Journal,* (Winter 1979):235 (hereafter cited as "Corporate Structure").

53.   Giebel, "Corporate Structure," 236.

54.   Brian Gill. Telephone interview with the author, 13 July 1983 (hereafter cited as Gill, 7/13); and Donald E. Sommer, "The Role of Open Shops in the Printing Industry." Internal memorandum to the membership of the Printing Industries of America, 26 January 1973, 3. (hereafter cited as Sommer)

55.   Joseph G. Correia, "Mergers in the Printing and Publishing Industries," *Printing and Publishing* (Fall 1968):8-12 (hereafter cited as "Mergers").

56.   William S. Lofquist, "Mergers and Acquisitions in the United States Printing and Publishing Industry," *Printing and Publishing* (Summer 1978):3, 7 (hereafter cited as "Mergers and Acquisitions").

57.   William S. Lofquist, "Shipments Concentration in the United States Printing and Publishing Industry," *Printing and Publishing* (Winter 1981/1982):3, 7 (hereafter cited as "Shipments Concentration").

58. Nelson Eldred, personal correspondence with the author, 8 April 1983 (hereafter cited as Eldred, 4/8). Eldred is technical director of the GATF.

59. U.S. Department of the Interior. U.S. National Resource Committee. *The Structure of the American Economy,* part I. (Washington, DC: GPO, 1939), 58; and U.S. Department of Commerce. *Printing and Publishing,* (October 1972):3.

60. Baker, *Displacement,* 14, 81.

61. Max Hall, ed., *Made in New York: Case Studies in Metropolitan Management* (Cambridge, MA: Harvard University Press, 1959), 147 (hereafter cited as *Metropolitan Management*); Baker, *Printing,* 19; and Seymour Lipset, Martin Trow, and James Coleman, *Union Democracy* (New York: The Free Press, 1956), 365 (hereafter cited as *Democracy*).

62. Gordon F. Bloom and Herbert R. Northrup, *Economics of Labor Relations* (Homeward, IL: Richard D. Irwin, 1981), 9 (hereafter cited as *Economics of Labor*); and Lipset, et al. *Democracy,* 235.

63. Giebel, "Corporate Structure," 237–8; and Jacob Loft, *The Printing Trades,* (New York: Farrar & Rinehart, 1944), 9–10, 168 (hereafter cited as *Trades*).

64. W. Eric Gustafson, "Printing and Publishing," in *Metropolitan Manufacturing,* Max Hall, ed., 233–4 (hereafter cited as "Printing").

65. Lipset, et al., *Democracy,* vii; and Munson, *Labor Relations,* 238–43.

66. Giebel, "Corporate Structure," 229–56.

67. N.Y.S. Department of Labor. *Labor Market Information Handbook for Occupational Planners and Administrators in New York State* (Albany, NY: N.Y.S. Department of Labor, 1980), 11.

68. Charles R. Cook, "Major Centers of Commercial Printing," *Printing and Publishing,* (Fall 1981):15 (hereafter cited as "Major Centers").

69. Courtney D. Gifford, ed., *AFL-CIO Membership Data: Directory of United States Labor Organizations,* 1982–83 ed., (Washington, DC: Bureau of National Affairs, 1982) 72–5 (hereafter cited as *AFL–CIO Data*); U.S. Department of Labor. *Union Wages,* 128.

70. Giebel, "Corporate Structure," 237; Gustafson, "Printing," 238–9; Leonard A. Drake, *Trends in the New York Printing Industry,* (New York: Columbia University Press, 1940), 32 (hereafter cited as *New York Printing*); John W. Seybold, *The Philadelphia Printing Industry* (Philadelphia, PA: The University of Pennsylvania Press, 1949), 14–15 (hereafter cited as *Philadelphia Printing*); and James E. Horne. Personal correspondence with the author, 16 April 1984.

71. Donald E. Sommer, "The Role of Open Shops in the Printing Industry." Internal memorandum to the membership of the Printing Industries of America, Inc., 26 January 1973, 3.

72. U.S. Department of Labor. Bureau of Labor Statistics. *Supplement to Employment and Earnings,* (Washington: GPO, July 1983), 185, 190; National Labor Relations Board. *Forty-Sixth Annual Report of the National Labor Relations Board for the Fiscal Year Ended September 30, 1981,* 169, 184; and Dennis Molloy. Telephone interview with the author, 1 July 1985.

73. Daniel Loftus. Telephone interviews with the author, 22 April and 8 May 1985. Loftus is director, human resources, Master Printers of America, Division of Printing Industries of America, Inc.

5

The ITU and GCIU Historical Case Studies

INTRODUCTION

Chapter 5 completes the analysis of the historical relations between technology, skill, union policy and craft membership that have developed since 1958. The test of the craft union membership model continues with the case studies of the ITU and GCIU.

This chapter tests the chronological relation between the reduction of skill, union response to technological change, and the decline in the memberships of the ITU and GCIU. These two case studies begin by reviewing the overall decline in union membership since 1969 and the actual displacement within the printing and typesetting market sectors. The potential displacement of the three primary printing crafts is then estimated on the basis of equipment-in-place surveys for 1958, trade literature, and expert opinion.

Finally, this chapter considers the relative influence of technology and union behavior upon the case studies of the ITU and GCIU within the context of each sector's distinct product characteristic. Since it has been established that the skill-reducing properties of new processes in typesetting, preparation, and press vary only in degree, given the consistent behavior of the ITU and GCIU, it can be expected that craft employment and membership will vary directly between printing and typesetting functions according to the skilled labor-displacing properties of new production equipment.

Table 5.1   Printing Union Membership 1955–83 (in thousands)

Union	1955	1957	1959	1961	1963	1965	1967	1969	1971	1973	1975	1977	1979	1981	1983
International Typographical Union (ITU)	78	78	79	81	86	87	90	89	87	81	73	61	52	47	43
Graphic Communications Union International (GCUI)*															154
International Printing & Graphic Communications Union (IPGCU)															
Printing Pressmen	87	92	96	99	100	100	102	106	107	104	105	99	94	93	
Stereotypers	12	12	12	12	12	11	10	9	8	7	(see note 3 below)	(see note 3 below)			
Graphic Arts International Union (GAIU)										99	93	83	77	74	
Photoengravers	16	16	16	15	(see note 1 below)										
Bookbinders	51	54	56	56	53	51	57	60	59	(see note 2 below)	(see note 2 below)				
Lithographers					30	43	45	46		(see note 2 below)	(see note 2 below)				
Total Union Membership	244	252	259	264	266	279	302	309	307	291	271	243	233	214	197

All unions arranged in the column below underwent a series of mergers and ultimately formed the GCUI. These mergers are detailed in notes 1–5.

Source: Clifford, Courtney D., ed., *AFL–CIO Membership Data: Directory of United States Labor Organizations*, 1984–85 ed. (Washington, DC: Bureau of National Affairs, 1984), 51–5.

Notes:

1. Merged into Lithographers and Photoengravers International Union, September 7, 1964.
2. Merged into Graphic Arts International Union, September 4, 1972.
3. Merged to form the International Printing and Graphic Communications Union, October 17, 1973.
4. American Lithographers Association (ALA) was disaffiliated with the AFL–CIO on August 21, 1958 and membership data is not included in the above Table.
5. IPGCU and GAIU merged on July 1, 1983 to form the graphic arts union, Graphic Communications International Union (GCIU).

* All unions arranged in the column below underwent a series of mergers and ultimately formed the GCUI. These mergers are detailed in notes 1–5.

123

UNION MEMBERSHIP DECLINE

Corresponding to the decline in the composite craft skill index, total printing union membership declined one-third in the 12 years after the peak of 309,000 members in 1969. This is summarized in Table 5.1. During this same period, 1969–83, commercial printing industry (SIC 275) production employment alone increased by 46,300.[1] Both of the two remaining national unions experienced membership declines as well. Total paid membership in the ITU declined from 89,000 to 43,000 during this period. Representing primarily preparation, press, and bindery workers, the GCIU declined from 220,000 to 154,000 between 1969 and 1983.

All ITU and GCIU membership are employed in the printing and publishing industry (SIC 27).[2] Union members are divided according to their employment in either the newspaper or commercial branch. Membership data in Table 5.1 include total union membership of both branches. On the basis of trade literature and expert opinion, commercial branch union membership will be separately estimated in the ITU and GCIU case studies.

Industry unionization is estimated for printing and publishing (SIC 27), commercial printing (SIC 275), and the competitive labor market. This is shown in Table 5.2. Unionization of all three different labor market definitions declined between 1959 and 1983. The most severe membership decline occurred in the competitive labor market. Including commercial, in-plant, and quick printers, union membership, as a percentage of total production workers, declined from 29 percent in 1958 to 10 percent in 1983.

The degree of unionization in in-house and quick printing plants is significantly less than that in commercial printing. In in-house plants, unionization is dependent upon whether or not the parent company is organized. Captive plants are usually oganized by white collar or the industrial union of the parent company's industry—and not graphic arts unions. The degree of unionization of in-house plants is only 15 percent based upon annual surveys of its membership. Mr. Llamas of the In-Plant Management Association believes this estimate is representative of the industry as a whole. The percentage of union organization in the quick printing industry is estimated by Robert L. Schweiger, former president of the National Association of Quick Printers, to be under 1 percent.[3]

The proportion of craftsmen as percentage of national union membership is not available for either the ITU or the GCIU. However, the proportional craft membership of New York City locals is available from Printing Industries of Metropolitan New York negotiator James

Table 5.2   **Relative Union Membership, 1958, 1970, 1980, and 1983** *(production workers)*

Membership Category	1958	1970	1980	1983
Printing and Publishing (SIC 27)				
Union Membership	255,000	308,000	223,500	197,000
Employment	563,000	679,000	698,900	710,200
Unionization—Industry	45%	45%	32%	28%
Commercial Printing (SIC 275)				
Commercial Branch				
Membership	120,900	154,450	110,400	99,200
Employment	220,300	274,600	307,300	319,900
Unionization—Industry	55%	56%	36%	31%
Competitive Labor Market				
Commercial Branch				
Membership	120,900	154,450	110,400	99,200
Employment	NA	542,350	801,677	860,497
Unionization—Labor Market	NA	29%	14%	12%

Source: Compiled by the author.

Notes:

1.   Competitive labor market estimate is from Table 3.10.

2.   Thirty-three percent of ITU membership in commercial printing is taken from *Typographical Journal,* published by the ITU, and reported in: "Selected Trends of the ITU," Special Studies Series, published by the Printing Industries of America, Inc.

3.   James E. Horne, industry negotiator and executive vice-president of the Printing Industry of New York, stated that approximately 36% of Printing and Graphic Communications membership was employed in commercial printing during an interview on 24 August 1983.

4.   Dennis Molloy, vice-president, Graphic Arts Employers of America, Printing Industries of America, Inc., advised during an interview on 6 May 1983 that about 80 percent of GAIU membership was employed in SIC 275, commercial printing.

5.   Annual union membership is the two-year average of prior and subsequent years.

E. Horne. The New York ITU Local No. 6 is estimated to have consisted of about 90 percent journeyman membership. Preparation and Printing Pressmen Local No. 51 has maintained a constant 75 percent ratio of craft as a percent of total membership since 1958. During the same period, 1958–83, journeymen accounted for a constant one-third of the GCIU Bindery 119B membership.[4]

ITU AND PHOTOCOMPOSITION: CASE STUDY NO. 1

The ITU case study begins with a review of the actual employment of skilled compositors and ITU members. After chronologically relating skill, craft employment, and union membership to photocomposition, this case study will consider the potential displacing power of CRT photocomposition.

Actual Labor Displacement

The actual commercial printing (SIC 275) labor displacement in composing room employment is seen to have occurred only in the craft occupations. Table 5.3 indicates that the employment of skilled typesetters declined by 12,970 from 31,450 to 18,480 in the ten years between 1970 and 1980. Unskilled composing room employment, however, increased by 1,100 during the same period.

Corresponding to the employment decline of 12,970 typesetting craftsmen, the ITU commercial branch membership decreased by 53 percent from 29,700 in 1967 to 14,190 in 1983.[5] This actual decline of 15,510 nearly equals the 12,970 decrease in craft composing room job opportunities presented in Table 5.3.

Restricting consideration to only union plants is an inadequate analytical framework when the effect of new processes is to shift production job opportunities outside the commercial printing industry. This study suggests that the effect of the new photocomposition process is to shift the production of typesetting and the demand for labor from commercial to in-house typesetting plants. Craftworker employment in commercial printing (SIC 275) declined by approximately 13,000 between 1970 and 1980 to a total of 18,000. This is shown in Table 5.3.

Yet, in 1978, in-house photocomposition plants substituted employment of 18,600 commercial printing industry typesetters. Private photocomposition plants employ an amount equal to 90 percent of the 20,680, (or 18,600) typesetters employed in SIC 275 during 1980 (Table 5.3). In-house typesetting employment is based upon the assumption that the average in-house and commercial plant employment is identical, and that in-house photocomposition installations equalled 90 percent of their commercial printing competitors (Table 5.4)

Table 5.3 Typesetting Estimated Employment in the Commercial Printing Industry SIC 275, 1970 and 1980 *(total employment)*

Occupational Category	Estimated Employment		
	1970	1980	Variation
Total Industry (SIC 275)	350,860	414,950	64,090
Craft Occupations			
Copy Cutters	190	320	
Hand Compositors	8,120	4,850	
Imposers and Make-up	4,090	1,570	
Linecasting Machine Operators	8,760	2,880	
Linecasting Keyboard Operators	1,010	730	
Ludlow Machine Operators	920	120	
Mark-up Men	680	—	
Monotype Casting and Keyboard	660	190	
Paste-up	2,320	2,870	
Photo-lettering Machine Operator	190	180	
Phototypesetting Machine/Key Operator	840	1,430	
Proofreader	3,670	3,340	
Total Craft Workers	31,450	18,480	(12,970)
Unskilled Occupations			
Phototypesetting Machine Monitor	—	390	
Phototypesetting Operator	180	1,040	
Linecasting Machine Tender*	—	550	
Strike-in Machine Operator	920	220	
Total Craft and Unskilled	32,550	20,680	(11,870)

Source: Compiled by the author.
* Hot type process only

Table 5.4 Commercial and Private Photocomposition Installations, 1978

Plant Size (Number of Employees)	Typesetting Plants	
	Commercial	In-Plant
1- 9	1,782	2,657
10-19	1,128	659
20-49	796	523
50-99	773	267
100 or more	597	440
Total	5,076	4,546

Source: Frank J. Romano, president, Graphic Arts Manufacturers' Association, Salem, New Hampshire. GATF Techno Economic Forecast 9, tables 1.3, 1.4.

Note: These tables were compiled by the author in combining the estimates of phototypesetting equipment-in-place with the estimates of multiterminal systems. As an index of relative employment, the distinction between single and multi-unit terminal systems is not significant.

Chronological Relation of Technology, Skill, and ITU Membership

Four years after its introduction, CRT photocomposition initiated the decline seen in the combined hot and cold skill indices. Since cold typesetting displaced hot casting, the combined skill index of both processes offers an appropriate measure of declining occupational craft skills. The membership data for the ITU in Table 5.5 excludes newspaper membership.

The typesetting craft skill index is calculated by multiplying the percent of industry occupational employment by the number of years training in each occupation. The composite typesetting skill index values are the sum of Table 3.4 hot and cold craft index values.

The typesetters craft skill index decreased by more than half between 1970 and 1980. During the same ten-year period, commercial industry craft employment and typesetting union membership declined by a similar amount. Table 5.5 indicates that craft typesetting employment declined by 12,970 and membership in the ITU by 14,000 between 1970 and 1981. The ITU commercial branch membership declined by 53 percent to a total of 14,190 in 1983.

Total Typesetting Production Employment in Table 5.5 consists of:

Industry	1970	1980
Commercial Printing (SIC 275)	31,450	18,480
In-plant Printing	9,000	18,600
	41,550	39,280

Private plant typesetting employment is based upon the 1978 distribution of photocomposition installations between commercial printers and private plants (Table 3.5). Assuming the average plant employment is identical in private and commercial plants, private plants employ 90 percent of available commercial typesetting employment data. Total employment distribution between private and commercial plants is assumed to be constant in 1970 and 1980. Industry expert Frank Romano, Editor of New England Printer and Publisher, stated that the number of photocomposition installations more than doubled between 1970 and 1980.

Potential Labor Displacement of Photocomposition

Potential displacement sets the limit and outlines the trend of a continuing process. The number of skilled handworkers potentially dis-

Table 5.5   Chronological Table of the Introduction of Photocomposition and the Variation in Typesetting Craft Skills, Competitive Employment, and ITU Commercial Branch Membership, 1967–83

Year	Skill Index	Employment		ITU Membership	Unionization
		Craftworkers	Total		
1967*	1.566	NA	NA	29,700	NA
1968	1.566	NA	NA	NA	NA
1969	1.566	NA	NA	29,400	NA
1970	1.037	31,450	41,550	NA	70%
1971	.970	NA	NA	28,700	NA
1972	.891	NA	NA	NA	NA
1973	.839	NA	NA	26,730	NA
1974	.760	NA	NA	NA	NA
1975	.692	NA	NA	24,100	NA
1976	.628	NA	NA	NA	NA
1977	.565	NA	NA	20,100	NA
1978	.526	NA	NA	NA	NA
1979	.503	NA	NA	17,200	NA
1980	.468	18,480	39,280	NA	42%
1981	NA	NA	NA	15,500	NA
1982	NA	NA	NA	NA	NA
1983	NA	NA	NA	14,200	NA

Source: Compiled by the author.
* Introduction of CRT photocomposition
Notes:
1.   Composing room occupations were classified into craft or other semiskilled occupations on the basis of functions that the union reserves for the exclusive jurisdiction of full journeymen. For instance, only a journeyman is permitted to set up a machine. A non-journeyman may operate a machine.
2.   Commercial branch is 33 percent of total ITU membership. ITU membership in commercial printing is taken from *Typographical Journal,* published by the ITU, and reported in: "Selected Trends of the ITU," Special Studies Series, published by the Printing Industries of America, Inc.
3.   Union membership is the two-year average of prior and subsequent years.

placed by photocomposition is difficult to estimate because of the continuously developing process capacity and wide variety of equipment designs. This section will subsequently establish the predominant use of traditional hot type skills in 1958, relate the years of craft training with the developing capability of cold type processes, and estimate the potential number of skilled handworkers displaced by CRT photocomposition.

Table 5.6 U. S. Printing and Allied Industries Composing Equipment-In-Place, 1958 (*firms employing 50 or more persons*)

Typesetting Machines	Total Survey
Traditional Metallic	
Linotype/Intertype	3,316
Monotype Keyboard	723
Pronotype Caster	1,135
Ludlow	616
Computer-Aided/Metallic	
Teletypesetter Perforator	235
Teletypesetter Caster	181
Computer-Aided/Nonmetallic	
Linofilm	10
Fotosetter	59
Photon	18
AFT Type Composing Machine	7
Establishments Reporting Cold Composition	
Equipment but not Included in the Above	106
Total Typesetting Machines	6,406

Source: Compiled by the author.
Notes:
1. Industries covered by the survey and their SIC codes for 1957 were: book printing (2732); commercial printing, except lithographic (2751); commercial printing, lithographic (2752); engraving and plate printing (2753); manifold business forms manufacturing (2761); greeting card manufacturing (2771); book binding (2789); typesetting (2791); photoengraving (2793); and electric typing and stereotyping (2794).

Out of the 22,596 establishments in the selected industries, 1634 of those surveyed accounted for 60% of the industry's total value of shipments.

2. Classification of equipment between traditional and transitional computer-aided and/or nonmetallic processes was based upon the author's knowledge of the industry and on descriptions of equipment presented in *The Printing Industry* by Victor Strauss (pp. 90–119, 132–3).

Evolution of Displacement

Until 1958, commercial typesetting was essentially the same art as it was in 1903 after the introduction of machinery or linotype casting. A U. S. Department of Commerce survey of composing room equipment-in-place confirms the predominance of the hot typesetting process. This process required traditional craft composing room skills. The Department of Commerce surveyed 1,634 of the 22,596 establishments in the selected printing and allied industries. These accounted for 60 percent of the surveyed industry's total value of shipments. This survey of composing equipment-in-place is limited to the larger firms employing 50 or more persons. Table 5.6 indicates that only 3 percent, or 200, of the 6,406 machines reported required other than traditional skills.

Photocomposition began to supplant hot metal typesetting in 1959 when nonunion employers of the Printing Industries of New York first began a craft training program for photocomposition. This program is detailed in Table 3.2. The *Census of Manufacturers* for 1963 began to evaluate photocomposition typesetting shipments. The seven digit census detail of specialized printing trades machinery (SIC 3555) permits the classification of typesetting machinery into either hot metal or photocomposition devices. Justifying typewriters are specifically excluded from specialized industry machinery shipments.

Specialized printing trades machinery (SIC 3555) value of product shipments measure the rate that new technology is incorporated into national printing production. New typesetting machinery shipments suggest that photocomposition began increasingly to displace hot type methods after it was first reported in 1963. An index of process substitution can be constructed by comparing the hot and cold type machinery shipments between 1963 and 1977. Table 5.7 summarizes the ratio of hot to cold type new machinery shipments.

Table 5.7 Ratio of Hot to Cold Typesetting New Machinery Shipments, 1963–77.

Year	Ratio Hot/Cold
1963	3.53
1967	1.40
1972	.35
1977	.03

Source: U. S. Department of Commerce. Bureau of the Census. "Seven Digit Value of Product Shipments of SIC 3555: Specialized Printing Trades Machinery," in *Census of Manufacturers.* Washington: GPO, 1977.

Notes:

1.   The annual value of specialized printing trades machinery (SIC 3555) was tabulated on the basis of seven-digit census detail. Production trades machinery that could not be classified were ignored either because there was insufficient description to allow proper tabulation or classification or because the machinery did not relate to lithographic (2752) or letterpress (2751) commercial printing production.

2.   Cold type machinery shipments were valuated according to the *Census of Manufacturers* for 1963. Sufficient product description permits the classification of typesetting machinery typewriters into either hot metal or photocomposition devices. Justifying typewriters were specifically excluded from specialized industry machinery shipments.

Expansion of Displacement

Since the beginning of its development in 1946, the potential of photocomposition to displace the skills of hot metal craftsmen has continually expanded. Due to this expanding capability, GATF stated that since 1968 the hot type process has lost ground to photocomposition. The first CRT photocomposition device was commercially installed in 1967. CRT digital photocomposition completely displaced the skilled compositors who set type and continually eroded job opportunities of the remaining craft make-up workers. Only ITU proofreaders' functions have not been directly displaced by photocomposition.[6]

In 1981, *The Seybold Report* surveyed worldwide multi-terminal system installations in commercial and newspaper plants. The survey indicated that there were 33 manufacturers of third generation equipment. In contrast, Barnett is able to use only the Mergenthaler Linotype as his basis of comparison with hand composition. Since the machine "exercised such a prominent influence," Barnett states "that attention may be confined to it without any danger of serious error."[7]

Elizabeth Baker estimated the potential displacement in the commercial pressroom after the introduction of automatic feeding machines. Potential displacement is estimated by separately calculating number of pressmen that could be employed if old and new model presses are operating at capacity during 1924 and 1929. Potential or "men theoretically employed are those who would have been according to collective bargaining agreement had all presses been running at capacity." Subsequently, Baker compared potential with actual displacement of manual feeders in New York City between 1924 and 1929.[8]

Notwithstanding the difficulties involved in an estimate of potential displacement, it is estimated that potentially more than three hot type craftsmen are displaced for each photocomposition operator employed. This study will suggest an estimate of potential displacement based upon expert opinion of the labor-displacing capabilities of new CRT photocomposition equipment in 1977. Mr. Nelson Eldred, technical director of the GATF, identified Frank J. Romano and John W. Seybold as the two foremost industry experts on photocomposition equipment. Each expert was asked to compare time standards necessary to set and compose three page sizes ($8\frac{1}{2}$ x 11", 6 x 9", $5\frac{1}{2}$ x $8\frac{1}{2}$") in both hot and cold type. As a rule of thumb, Romano stated that a CRT photocomposition operator can produce two or three times the amount of matter as his hot type counterpart. Seybold stated that an increase in photocomposition productivity of two or three times is too conservative and applicable chiefly to financial typesetting because of the percentage of copy revisions. Depending upon the repetitiveness of copy and format, a photocomposition operator can produce up to 100 times the amount of composition in directory work as his hot type counterpart.[9]

Industry expert Romano's statement that only 10 percent of private plants in 1978 operated electronic photocomposition equipment suggests that the shift of typesetting outside of the commercial printing industry will continue.[10] Photocomposition has shifted employment demand to in-house typesetting plants by altering the skill, cost, and equipment operating environments. Office secretaries and typists are able to keyboard, edit, file, and store text without knowledge of typography. Costs are reduced by integrating data and word processors with phototypesetting equipment and by eliminating the need for rekeyboarding and proofreading. Speed and security are added advantages of in-house typesetting. Instead of the antiquated, mechanical linotype machine situated on the factory floor, typesetting is now performed in a clean office environment.

GRAPHIC COMMUNICATIONS INTERNATIONAL UNION AND PHOTO-DIRECT AND ELECTROSTATIC PROCESSES: CASE STUDY NO. 2

A second test of the hypothesis that craft union membership declined in direct proportion to both the decline in the need for craft skills, and union resistance to skill reduction is seen in the historical case study of the Graphic Communications International Union (GCIU) between 1958 and 1983. The significant shift in production outside the commercial printing industry, the entirely unskilled operation of the new processes, and the continuing character of process development are factors that will all be considered in this case study. However, factors considered by Baker and Barnett, such as the restriction of trade entry and usefulness of skills, will not be considered here. The GCIU case study will now first consider the paradox of declining union membership during a period of increasing craft employment.

A Brief History of the Union

The GCIU is the largest union in the printing industry and represents all printing production functions except those within the ITU jurisdiction of composition. The GCIU was formed on July 1, 1983 by a merger of the pressmen and bindery unions. The pressmen's union was previously named the International Printing and Graphic Communications Union (IPGCU) and the former bindery union was named the Graphic Arts International Union (GAIU).[11] The successive mergers and membership figures of the representative unions are outlined in Table 5.1.

The crafts of the new GCIU's membership declined less rapidly than the compositors' during the period under study. Membership, in what was commonly called the pressmen's union, declined from 48,500 in 1968 to 44,000 in 1983. Bindery union membership had by this time declined by 38,000 from its 1969 total of 168,000 in commercial printing. These, too, are indicated in Table 5.1.

The demand for bindery labor depends on the location of the prior printing production stage—the pressroom. Thus, the decline in industry bindery employment is directly proportional to the decline in union pressrooms. In particular, this is seen in the decline in commercial printing bindery production employment from a total of 43,640 in 1970 to 39,110 in 1980. The total employment decline figure of 4,530 is composed of 420 craft and 4,110 semiskilled bindery workers. These figures are shown in Table 5.8.

Binderies, as adjuncts of the pressroom, are dependent upon compositors and pressmen for their union membership. The bindery is normally organized at the invitation and with the support of the compositors and pressmen and is rarely organized in a shop where both compositors and pressmen are nonunion.[12]

Since the bookbinder's craft has remained largely unchanged since 1958, their declining union membership will not be separately considered from that of the pressmen. The five-year apprenticeship of a bookbinder has not been altered by technological change. However, technological change has reduced union membership by shifting the semiskilled bindery functions of cutting, collating, punching, and stitching outside of the traditional sphere of union influence into in-plant and quick printers.

Potential Displacement

The vulnerability of commercial printers to photo-direct and electrostatic processes and to substitute suppliers of standard, short-run, single-color printed matter is clear when one reviews the 1958 and 1960 surveys of presses in place. The type of printed matter produced on new direct-image plates, A. B. Dick press equipment, or electrostatic printers was formerly produced on sheet-fed equipment of less than 14 x 20" maximum sheet size. Table 5.9 indicates that small press equipment comprised 45 percent of all presses in the commercial printing industry's establishments of 20 employees or more. In fact, the industry proportion of small press equipment is probably higher than 28 percent since the nonsurveyed printer with less than 20 employees utilizes small equipment.

Surveys of press equipment in place support the premise that traditional craft skills exclusively are required at the beginning of the period under study. None of the primary skill-reducing innovations listed in Table 2.1 are reported in the surveys of commercial printers made in 1958 and 1960. The survey taken in 1958 is confined to 1,634 establishments employing 50 or more persons. This survey shows that these establishments accounted for 60 percent of the total value of products shipped. The second survey of letterpress and lithographic establish-

Table 5.8   Preparation, Press and Bindery Employment, Commercial Printing Industry, SIC 275, 1970 and 1980 *(total employment)*

Occupational Category	Estimated Employment		
	1970	1980	Variation
Total Industry	350,860	414,950	64,090
Preparation Occupations			
Cameraman	5,640	10,980	
Developers	680	—	
Platemakers	5,090	7,130	
Strippers	7,470	14,780	
Total Preparation	18,880	32,890	14,010
Pressroom Occupations			
Pressmen: Letterpress,			
Sheet and Roll	22,500	17,370	
Pressmen: Offset			
Sheet and Roll	26,500	53,280	
Press Assistants and Feeders			
(Semiskilled)	16,340	17,230	
Total Pressroom	65,340	87,880	22,540
Bindery Occupations			
Binding Machine: Set-Up Men	5,310	6,220	
Bookbinder: Hand	3,250	1,920	
Bindery Workers (Semiskilled)	35,080	30,970	
Total Bindery	43,640	39,110	4,530
Total Preparation, Press and Bindery Categories	127,860	159,880	32,020

Source: Compiled by the author.
Note:
Classifications and groupings of commercial printing industry occupations are made on the basis of the author's experience.

ments covered 1,497 plants employing 20 to 49 persons. This sample accounted for 25 percent of industry value of products shipped.[13]

The minor innovations of automatic equipment designed to expose and develop plates, and to control register partially displaced manual craft skills. These had the effect of decreasing the term of preparation and press apprenticeships as is indicated in Table 3.2. Most important, the major innovations of electrostatic and photo-direct processes totally displaced the skills of the preparation and press craft worker.

Chronological Relation of Technology, Skill, and Membership in the GCIU

Paradoxically, while craft employment increased, membership in the GCIU steadily declined after 1969. In contrast to the typesetters, trade preparation and press craft employment show an increase during the ten years after 1970. Preparation craft employment alone shows an increase of 14,010 during this period. Table 5.8 indicates the increase in press employment. This category increased by 22,540 during these same ten years. Chapter 3 demonstrates that the increase in the demand for

Table 5.9   Presses In-Place, U. S. Printing and Allied Industries, 1960 *(establishments with 20 or more employees)*

Press Size*	Total Letterpress and Lithographic Presses in Survey	
Small Sheet-fed Presses:		
Platen (all)	7,871	
Flat Bed Cylinder (22 x 29")*	2,606	
Lithographic (22 x 30")	2,315	
	12,792	(45%)
Larger Sheet-fed and All Roll-		
fed Presses	15,256	(55%)
Total Presses in Place	28,048	(100%)

Source: U. S. Department of Commerce. Bureau of the Census. "Letterpress and Lithographic Printing Presses in Place in the United States by State and Region," by Charles R. Cook and Theodore C. Collins, in *Printing and Publishing Industry Report.* Washington: GPO, 1964

* Dimensions indicate maximum sheet size

Notes:

1. Press equipment was classified according to the total amount of such equipment in both short- and long-run categories. These data were developed on the basis of the author's experience.

2. One-half of the cylinder and lithographic minimum size sheet-fed presses with a maximum size of 22 x 30" were included in these data.

full-color printing, a demand driven by the decline in relative unit cost, is the explanation of the increase in skilled preparation and press employment. Yet, Table 5.10 indicates that while craft employment increased, membership in the GCIU declined from 129,000 in 1970 to 62,000 in 1980. This inverse relation between skilled employment and craftworker membership in the GCIU, as well as the lack of evidence establishing management conversion of union to open shops, requires additional explanation of the increase in nonunion craft employment.

Total preparation, press and bindery production employment in Table 5.10 consists of:

Industry	1970	1980
Commercial Printing (SIC 275)	127,860	156,880
In-plant Printers	358,160	454,960
Quick Printers	2,590	24,494
	488,610	636,334

Table 5.10 Chronological Table Relating Electrostatic and Photo-Direct Process Introduction to the Variation in Craft Skills, Competitive Employment, and GCIU Commercial Branch Membership, 1959–83

Year	Skill Index	Employment Craftworkers	Total	GCIU Membership	Unionization
1959 *	NA	NA	NA	96,500	NA
1960	NA	NA	NA	NA	NA
1961	NA	NA	NA	96,800	NA
1962 †	NA	NA	NA	NA	NA
1963	NA	NA	NA	82,700	NA
1964	NA	NA	NA	NA	NA
1965	NA	NA	NA	104,800	NA
1966	3.852	NA	NA	NA	NA
1967	3.852	NA	NA	120,300	NA
1968	3.852	NA	NA	NA	NA
1969	2.568	NA	NA	125,400	NA
1970	2.117	76,440	488,610	NA	0.26
1971	2.180	NA	NA	125,400	NA
1972	2.240	NA	NA	NA	NA
1973	2.304	NA	NA	119,200	NA
1974	2.340	NA	NA	NA	NA
1975	2.427	NA	NA	112,200	NA
1976	2.484	NA	NA	NA	NA
1977	2.564	NA	NA	102,000	NA
1978	2.597	NA	NA	NA	NA
1979	2.630	NA	NA	95,400	NA
1980	2.657	103,490	636,334	NA	0.15
1981	NA	NA	NA	92,700	NA
1982	NA	NA	NA	NA	NA
1983	NA	NA	NA	85,000	NA

Source: Compiled by the author.

* Introduction of Electrophotography
† Introduction of Photo-Direct Offset (copy to plate)

COMPARATIVE CASE STUDIES OF THE ITU AND GCIU

The craft union membership model implies that union resistance to skill reduction allows nonunion plants to continually increase their proportion of commercial printing industry employment. Specifically, the GCIU maintains a higher relative skilled wage rate as well as prevents the substitution of specialized operators for craftworkers. This section will establish the greater specialization of printing and binding labor in nonunion plants, further increasing relative union labor costs, and explains the distinct outcome of the ITU and GCIU case studies.

Compared with the typesetting sector, craftworker employment in the GCIU increased while the unionization of skilled workers declined. Table 5.5 indicates that craftworker unionization in the typesetting sector remained at a relatively constant 92 percent and 88 percent between 1969 and 1980 respectively. All things being equal, one would expect craftworker unionization to either remain constant or to decline together with skilled employment. In the sector dominated by the GCIU, one sees craftworker employment increase while the proportion of skilled printers belonging to the GCIU actually declines. It is the rise in demand for craft-intensive color printing that accounts for the increase in skilled employment in the nontypesetting sector. In addition to demonstrating the decline in unit cost and the rise in demand for full-color printing, Chapter 3 also establishes the segmentation in the product markets that shields the ITU and GCIU from competition from in-plant and quick printers in the production of complex printed matter.

Nonunion plants compete against union printers with significantly lower labor cost. Table 4.6 and 4.7 indicate that both the ITU and GCIU relative union/nonunion craftworker wages increased between 1958 and 1982. While national skilled wage data are not available, comparable wage rates are available for trades dominated by the ITU and GCIU in New York City. Horne, the management representative who negotiated the contracts summarized in Table 5.11, states that the relative wage rates dramatically understate the wage union/nonunion labor cost differential. After considering union benefits, "the non-union employer pays the New York City craftworker 30-40% less." Confirming the relatively higher union craftworker labor cost, the president of the national union employers' association estimated that skilled nonunion labor is paid 25 percent less than their union counterparts. Both Horne and Solomon attribute the decline in the proportion of union craftworkers to the higher relative cost of ITU and GCIU labor.[14]

What distinguishes the experience of the ITU and GCIU is the ability of nonunion plants in the printing sector to reorganize the work process in order to significantly reduce labor cost. The work rules of the

Table 5.11 Ratio of Hourly Wages of Union and Nonunion Craftsmen in New York City, 1958–82

Year	Typesetting	Preparation	Press (One-color)	(Two-color)
1958	1.10	1.02	1.05	1.06
1959	1.09	1.03	1.04	1.06
1960	1.09	1.05	1.04	1.05
1961	NA	NA	NA	NA
1962	1.15	1.06	1.05	NA
1963	1.11	1.06	1.06	1.07
1964	1.14	1.05	1.05	1.07
1965	1.12	1.08	1.09	1.08
1966	1.13	1.11	1.11	1.08
1967	1.16	1.08	1.07	1.03
1968	1.15	1.10	1.11	1.04
1969	1.14	1.10	1.11	1.04
1970	1.24	1.12	1.04	1.02
1971	1.27	1.14	1.16	1.14
1972	1.34	1.19	1.21	1.19
1973	NA	NA	NA	NA
1974	1.29	1.15	1.17	1.16
1975	1.20	1.16	1.16	1.15
1976	1.23	1.19	1.20	1.19
1977	1.26	1.17	1.18	1.17
1978	1.32	1.17	1.18	1.17
1979	1.39	1.18	1.20	1.19
1980	1.47	1.17	1.21	1.17
1981	1.42	1.23	1.23	1.21
1982	1.46	1.24	1.25	1.24

Source: Compiled by the Author.

GCIU prohibit the substitution of craftworkers with lower paid, specialized machine operators. The respective processes in typesetting and printing require a different degree of craftworker involvement. If we divide each function into set-up and operation, then the increased opportunity for work reorganization in the printing sector is apparent. The typesetting of complicated mathematical and tabular matter requires a craftworker to set-up and operate equipment. Complex typesetting requires continuous operator decision making despite the skill-reducing properties of photocomposition.

In contrast to the typesetting sector, nonunion plants in the GCIU sector can substantially reduce the cost of operation by a division of labor not permitted in union shops. New press and bindery electronic machines control speed set-up and, most importantly, have increased the capability of nontypesetting sector equipment to monitor and self-adjust its own operation. Chapter 3 details the evolution of electronic press control equipment. In open plants, skilled labor only sets-up press and bindery equipment, while lower paid labor, with machine specific skills, monitors equipment operation. The GCIU sector permits the division of labor because of the relatively larger lot size in printing and binding. In typesetting, one operator might produce two or three complex pages during a seven-hour shift. In typesetting, the lot size is one page since each page is unique. In the sector dominated by the GCIU, the typical commercial printing lot size is 5,000 to 10,000 units. After set-up, a lower-skilled press monitor can print or bind between 5,000 and 10,000 units per hour, depending upon the machinery used and specific job requirements.

Contracts negotiated by the GCIU require craftworkers to both set-up and operate printing equipment. For example, the contract for Local No. 51 of the Pressmen's Union in New York City indicates that each press must be operated by at least one journeyman. The contract for Local No. 119B-43B of the Bindery Union indicates that only a journeyman may operate automatically fed folding and stitching equipment in addition to cutters.[15]

Expert opinion confirms that press and bindery technology permits a lower proportion of skilled labor in nonunion plants than their union counterparts. Horne and Molloy indicate that nonunion employers seldom use skilled labor for tasks other than set-up and running difficult work. Horne indicates that nonunion press and bindery plants in New York City are able to realize lower labor cost by having one journeyman set-up and oversee the operation of many pieces of equipment on the same shift. Simich confirms the nationwide trend to use lesser-skilled personnel instead of craft labor to monitor the operation of bindery equipment. Molloy states that union plants nationwide are required by contract to employ a significantly higher proportion of skilled workers than their nonunion counterparts.[16]

An example of the difference in the proportion of craftworkers as well as total manning between union and nonunion plants is given by the National Association of Printers and Lithographers (NAPL). On the basis of manufacturers' specifications, NAPL compared the manning in 1972 with the 1982 press model. The 1972 Miehle-Roland 55″ six-color operated at speeds of 6,500 impressions per hour (IPH) and required a crew of four. The 1982 model capable of speed to 10,000 IPH needs a crew of three. A smaller 50″ six-color press in GCIU Local 51 requires a crew of four with two craftsmen. As an option, the employer may operate with only three men—but all must be craftsmen. Industry expert Coulson states that the 1982 model only requires one craftsman. As another instance, in 1982 Local 51 requires one press craftworker for every two on-line web printing units—regardless of the work or equipment manufacturers' specifications.[17]

As an indication of greater nonunion plant specialization, education expert Simich indicates that nonunion apprenticeship tends to be more specialized and machine specific. During an interview, the executive director of the Printing Industries of Metropolitan New York confirmed these indications of the trend toward more specialized training. He states:

> During the last five (5) or ten (10) years this trend has been for the individual to serve his entire apprenticeship in two (2) years on a very specialized piece of equipment and not on all the various types of equipment within each bindery. . . . [In fact], training has become more specialized in preparation, press and bindery areas. In contrast to the fifties and sixties, rarely has an apprentice trained on all equipment within a function of a particular plant.[18]

Forms and Effects of GCIU Displacement

The GCIU experiences two forms of displacement. In both, the interaction of technology and union behavior are required to explain each form of displacement. In-plant and quick printers substitute unskilled labor in the production of relatively simple printed matter. Nonunion printers in the commercial printing industry displace skilled union membership in the production of complex printing and binding.

It is technological change, together with union resistance to unskilled processes, that cause noncomplex printing to shift outside the commercial printing industry. The potential displacement of the preparation, press, and bindery operators of the GCIU took the form of job opportunities lost to private and quick printers. These substitute suppliers organize their production around direct-image platemaking, electrostatic printers, and small press equipment. (See Chapter 2 for a discussion of this equipment.) Due to the limitations of equipment, in-plant and quick printers usually limit their production to standard size, single-color printed matter in quantities under 1,000 impressions. The growth in quick and in-house plant employment approximates the number of job opportunities lost by the GCIU. Table 3.6 indicates that between 1958 and 1983, there was an increase in production employment at private plants of 96,800. At quick printing plants, the increase in the number of production workers was 21,904.

Specialization of GCIU sector production permits an increase in the proportion of unskilled workers not reflected in the occupational employment data of Table 5.10. Rather than training an apprentice in the three functions of camera, platemaking, and stripping, specialization permits a few craft workers to direct the unskilled in preparation work. Work rules, however, still require a journeyman. Technology, as previously demonstrated, has reduced the platemaking function to the level of the unskilled. As an illustration, the specialization of preparation labor would permit the 7,130 unskilled platemakers employed in 1980 to assist the 10,980 cameramen and 14,780 strippers also employed at that time. In addition, the division of camera and stripping into skilled and unskilled functions, such as the processing of non-register line work, further reduces the proportion of skill in the preparation department.

While it is difficult to distinguish between the influence of technology and that of union policy, it appears that in the case of the ITU, technology is the primary explanation of membership decline. As a percentage of the total ITU typesetting sector, craftworker employment declined from 76 to 47 percent while craftworker unionization remained at 92 and 88 percent between 1970 and 1980 (see Table 5.5). The ITU contributed to membership decline by blocking the introduction of photocomposition in union plants, as well as by demonstrating an unwillingness or inability to organize the unskilled new process operators.

In the case of the GCIU, it appears that union policy is more significant than the influence of technology. Craftworker employment in the nontypesetting sector remained at a constant 16 percent of the competitive labor market. The increase in color printing more than compensated for the deskilling influence of new processes. Table 5.10 indicates that the growth of craftworker employment in the printing sector was 27,050 between 1970 and 1980. GCIU resistance to skill displacement increased the relative union labor cost and encouraged the shift of craft production to nonunion commercial printing industry plants.

FUTURE TRENDS IN TECHNOLOGY AND UNIONIZATION

The enforcement of the journeyman rule during the last 25 years has shifted unskilled production outside the commercial printing industry and craftworker employment to nonunion plants within the industry. Technological change continues to erode the remaining craft job opportunities in union plants. Over the years ahead, the relative cost of the journeyman rule will continue to encourage increased competition from substitute, nonunion suppliers. Competition in the product market clearly illustrates the ease with which the substitution of unskilled for craft labor can be achieved.[19] Contractual relations, together with the power to strike, cannot isolate union labor from long-range competitive pressures by the new processes.

The survival of the ITU and GCIU is dependent upon recognition of not only the historic, but also of the continuing deskilling of printing production. The effect of photocomposition on Typographical, the oldest and most powerful printing union, is transparent. What is not obvious, however, is the effect of technology on the crafts of preparation, press, and bindery workers. Masking the effect of skill reduction through technological innovation is the increased demand for color printing and the introduction of substitute processes outside of the commercial printing industry. Color printing requires craft skills and conventional methods. The increased demand for color printing has, in turn, increased the demand for these craft skills. Aside from the possibility that tastes might change away from color production, nonconventional printing processes are quickly expanding their color reproduction capabilities.

The continual introduction of new processes will therefore continually reduce the skills required of the average worker and alter the total industry employment proportion of union and nonunion workers. Consequently, technology threatens to destroy the remaining craft functions just as photocomposition has obsolesced the typesetter's craft. Specifically, the expanding capability of new processes in digitization, electrostatic, and duplicator reproduction will complete the process of skill reduction throughout the printing plant. While there will always exist highly-skilled craftsmen, both their numbers and the skills of their assistants will be drastically reduced.

The most significant threat to craftsmen is the process of digitization, the process of capturing and transforming images into discrete whole numbers and thereby rendering them capable of electronic manipulation. Photocomposition was the first application of this process in the printing industry. This process permits the manipulation of keyboard strokes into a completed page. However, the text is a small part of the imagery or information environment. Intricate craft processes and cost barriers inherent in reproducing images have made text matter more efficient to print than pictures.[20]

With the expansion in the capacity of digitization to the integration of text with images in single- and process-color printing, technology will further erode the need for craft skills. The eventual application of this process would be in the electronic scanning of text and images, thereby manipulating the binary data into proofs and press plates. Furthermore, the digitization of images permits the printing press computer console operator to compensate, through adjustments in ink and fountain solutions, for discrete variances in press output and the desired image.

L. W. Wallis predicts that by the end of the 1980s new technology will accelerate the displacement of the only printing occupations that have continually and significantly increased since 1970 (indicated in Table 3.9). The preparation and press craft occupations will be displaced by electronic printing and computer-to-plate systems. The next dramatic step in technology will come, according to Wallis, in the end product of the phototypesetting process. Presently, this process creates an intermediate image contributing to the finished print. The phototypeset output is frequently used to produce one or two intermediaries, that is, a film positive/negative and printing plate. Electronic printers and direct computer-to-plate systems bypass the need for both these photographic intermediaries and the printing process. Special interest publications, as well as financial and scholarly printing, are mentioned by Wallis as current applications of electronic printers. Direct computer-to-plate systems are increasingly applicable to all other larger-run commercial printing.[21]

Image scanners are other manifestations of the trend toward digitization of the printing craft functions. In 1979, it was estimated that 2,500 scanners were in use and were expected to double by 1983. Because of their cost, process color scanners will probably be limited to larger shops. Single-color scanners, however, are within the reach of most printers. In 1979 color scanners cost between $200,000 and $500,000; black and white image processors, however, started at $15,000.[22]

While digitization threatens the craft skills of color printers, electrostatic processes are eroding the short-run, single-color market for the traditional offset and letterpress processes. Since the introduction of the office copier in 1959, the capability of electrophotography has expanded rapidly. Despite the introduction of the Xerox 5600 color copier in 1974, the imaging characteristics of xerography were, by 1978, still limited to the reproduction of line copy and text material. By 1984, electrostatic printing began to reproduce coarse continuous-tone pictures. Schaffert predicts: "Now we come to tomorrow. In the future I predict that xerography will become more a part of commercial printing, particularly in the short end of the market, for runs up to 10,000 or less."[23]

SUMMARY

These two case studies support the importance of both technology and union behavior as determinants of craft union membership. Both membership in the ITU and craft employment decline by a similar amount after the introduction in 1967 of CRT photocomposition. Despite an increase in skilled printing sector employment following the increase in demand for full-color printing, membership in the GCIU declined by half between 1969 and 1983. The maintenance of ITU and GCIU skilled wage rates prevent the recruitment of unskilled new process operators despite the introduction of partial and complete skill displacing technologies. Taking advantage of the larger unit production in the nontypesetting sector, technological change enables nonunion firms to significantly reduce labor cost through a division of labor and the substitution of specialized semiskilled and unskilled labor for printing and bindery craftworkers.

CONCLUSION

This study demonstrates that the decline in the memberships of the ITU and GCIU between 1969 and 1983 was caused by technological skill displacement as well as by the responses of printing unions to new production processes. The craft union membership model, presented in Chapter 1, incorporates both technology and trade union behavior as the determinants of membership in both the ITU and GCIU. This membership model shows how exogenous technology begins the chain of events that determine the proportion of skilled and unskilled production workers. The second determinant, trade union behavior, alters the number of jobs under union contract by policies that determine the operator qualifications, expand membership to the unskilled, and organize nonunion workers. Economic literature suggests a third determinant of union membership decline—management resistance. Chapter 4 considers and then rejects this variable because there is no data to establish an increase in management resistance to unionization efforts of the ITU and GCIU between 1958 and 1983. However, while the evidence presented is inconsistent with the competing explanation of membership decline, it is not sufficient to disprove the management resistance hypothesis.

Memberships of the ITU and GCIU initially began to decline in 1969 because new production technology required a continually lower level of operator skill. The ITU represents typesetters and the GCIU represents preparation, press and bindery workers. This study develops support for the hypothesis in the decline in the number of years of craft training required, the development of the composite printers' craft index, and the relative employment growth of unskilled printers.

The decline in training requirements following the introduction of advanced technology establishes the influence of new processes on craft skills. Craft apprenticeship is the source of specialized production skills and serves as a measure of these skills. Between 1948 and 1982, in both union and nonunion apprenticeships, there was a reduction in the number of years' training required for typesetters, preparation workers, and press craftsmen. The decline in the length of craft training required for all printers except the bindery craftworker was examined. Concurrent with the substitution of photocomposition for traditional hot type methods, non-union typesetting training began to decline from 6 years in 1958 to 1 year in 1978. The decline of 2 years in preparation and 3 years in nonunion press training since 1958 primarily reflects both the mechanization of hand operations and the increased use of automatic control devices.

Additional support for the first hypothesis, which states that new production technology reduces the level of craft skill required in printing production, is also found in the composite printers' skill index. This index measures the decline in printing craft skills. Training is a measure of skill. Within each stage of production, the craft index is calculated by multiplying the years of nonunion apprenticeship by the comparable percent of industry occupational employment. Coincident with the introduction of CRT photocomposition and the automation of hand preparation of press skills between 1966 and 1980, the index indicates a one-third reduction in skill.

While this printers' skill index measures the partial displacement of craftworker skills, a different measure is required to support the existence of complete skill displacement. An indication of the displacement of craftworkers is the relative employment growth of unskilled printers. While photocomposition reduces the typesetter's craft apprenticeship from 6 years to only 1 year, electrostatic and photo-direct offset printing entirely displace the skills of the preparation and press craftsmen. Manufacturers of photo-direct offset and electrostatic printing equipment state that only unskilled labor is required to operate their equipment. Process competition from photo-direct offset and electrostatic printing comes primarily from private and quick printers who substitute for commercial printers.

Table 3.13 supports the second hypothesis and establishes that the craftworkers as a percent of production labor in the competitive printing industry has declined from 20 to 16 percent between 1970 and 1980. It is hypothesized that simplified new processes have reduced the demand for craftworkers employed in the typesetting and printing sectors of the labor market. Craftworkers, as a percent of the total typesetting labor market, declined from 75 to 47 percent between 1970 and 1980—3 years after the first commerical introduction of CRT photocomposition.

Contrary to expectation, proportional employment of preparation, press, and bindery craftworkers actually increased from 13 to 14 percent between 1970 and 1980. Counteracting the substitution of unskilled for craftworkers is the increase in the demand for craft intensive full-color printing. Full-color printing still requires preparation and press craftworkers utilizing traditional four-color lithographic processes. After compensating for the increase in color printing, nontypesetting craftworker proportional employment is seen to decline from 14 to 12 percent during the same ten year period. Composition and bindery workers in the two bracketing stages of production are unaffected by an increase in the demand for color printing.

The major cause for the increased demand for full-color printing is the reduction in unit costs between 1967 and 1984. The data presented, supported by expert opinion and trade literature, indicate this increase in the demand for full-color printing. It was shown that the unit cost for full-color printed matter relative to non-full-color work has declined by half between 1965 and 1984.

The relative earnings of printing production workers also tests the hypothesized existence of craft decline. It is expected that both the decline in the level of skill as well as proportion of skilled workers will cause a reduction of printers' earnings relative to manufacturing production workers as a whole. It is established that printers' relative hourly earnings declined from 1.17 in 1958 to 1.06 in 1983. This decline in the printers' relative earnings only began after the reduction in the craft skill index in 1967. In the 10 years prior to the decline in the craft skills index, relative earnings were constant.

However, the aggregate measure of printing production earnings includes a significant decline in the proportion of higher paid union printers. Instead of measuring both a decline in the level of craft and an increased proportion of nonskilled labor, it can be argued that variation in relative earnings only registers the decline in labor market unionization. While national nonunion industry wage data are not available, such data are available for craftworkers in New York City between 1958 and 1982.

The historical trend of New York City nonunion skilled printers' relative earnings is consistent with the variation of total printing industry production wages. The trend in the relative earnings of skilled nonunion printers is a more direct measure of the influence of craft decline on skilled printing wages. Relative wages continued to increase before the reduction in apprenticeship training. The number of years' craft training, as well as the printers' skill index, began to decline in 1969. Nationwide, printers' relative earnings began to decline in 1973. In New York City, the relative earnings of skilled printers began their decline in

1975-76. The interval between the decline in training after 1969 and the decline in relative earnings was 4 years for all industry workers and 6 to 7 years for nonunion craft workers in New York City.

The craft union membership model incorporates union behavior as a second determinant of membership. It identifies the journeyman work rule as the primary union response to both the decline in the level of craft skills as well as the substitution of unskilled labor in traditional craft functions. The journeyman work rule requires that craftsmen operate any new equipment able to perform journeyman functions at rates of pay and terms of employment equivalent to those of superseded craftworkers.

The craft union membership model presented in the last set of hypotheses explains the influence of labor union policies. The third hypothesis, for example, states that both the ITU and GCIU have maintained relative skilled membership wages in response to a decline in the level of craft skill. Confirming expectations, it is demonstrated that the ratio of skilled union wages to all manufacturing production workers climbed from 1.53 in 1968 to 1.63 in 1980. In the 10 years prior to 1968, relative skilled union wage rates remained constant while membership increased.

The third hypothesis implies that the application of work rules prevents the recruitment of unskilled, new process operators into union plants under the jurisdiction of the ITU and GCIU. After establishing the continued existence of the journeyman work rule, this hypothesis is supported with an estimation of the incremental cost of this rule, as well as of the decline in the proportion of union operators after new process introduction. The incremental cost of this rule is estimated to be nearly double the market wage in the photocomposition, photo-direct offset, and electrostatic processes. Table 4.2 presents the incremental wage cost of the printers' work rule in 1959 and in 1982. In addition, Table 4.3 indicates that membership in the ITU declined as a proportion of the competitive labor market from 51 percent in 1970 to 21 percent in 1980. Membership in the ITU declined despite relatively constant total typesetting employment. Increasing preparation and press craft employment did not stop the decline from 26 to 10 percent in the proportion of operators who were members of the GCIU between 1970 and 1980.

Chapter 5 examines the interaction of technological change and union policies in the two historical case studies of the ITU and GCIU. To this end, it is shown how both craft employment opportunities and membership in the ITU declined by a similar amount after the introduction of CRT photocomposition in 1967; employment of skilled typesetters declined by 12,970 from 31,450 in 1970 to 18,480 in 1980. Paralleling the decline in employment, membership in the commercial branch of the ITU declined by 14,000 during the same period.

The craft decline hypothesis is tested by chronologically relating skill reduction, craft employment, and membership in the GCIU. In order to so test this hypothesis, this chapter presents a case study of the GCIU which first considers the paradox of declining union membership and increasing craft employment during the decade of the 1970s. Preparation and press craft employment increased by 36,790 during this decade. Chapter 3 demonstrates that the increase in demand for multicolor printing causes the increase in demand for preparation and press craft workers.

The significance of the variables of technological change and union behavior itself varies between the case studies of the ITU and GCIU. Of the two determinants, technological change appears to be the most important in the case of ITU; union behavior is the major determinant in the case of the GCIU. In the typesetting sector of the ITU, the decline of 14,000 in craftworker emloyment is almost identical to the reduction in membership in the ITU. As anticipated, the unionization of craftworkers remained relatively constant at 92 percent in 1970 and 88 percent in 1980.

While there is a decline in the proportion of the members of the ITU who are typesetting craftworkers, quite a different outcome occurs in the case study of the GCIU. There, despite the proportional increase in craftworker employment from 15 percent in 1970 to 16 percent in 1980, union membership in the competitive labor market sector of the GCIU declines by two-thirds. Given the limitation of craftworkers in the commercial printing industry and the increase in craft-intensive, full-color printing which led to a greater employment of skilled labor established in Chapter 3, a second variable is necessary to explain the decline in printing sector craft worker unionization.

Chapter 4 establishes the relative union/nonunion labor cost as the major determinant of the decline in the union membership in the GCIU. Data is presented that indicate that relative union wages increased in both the typesetting and printing labor market sectors. What distinguishes the two labor market sectors is the ability of nonunion firms in the printing sector to reorganize production and thereby dramatically reduce the proportion of craftworkers as well as the average labor cost per hour. Complex typesetting requires craftworkers to both set-up and operate equipment. However, nonunion firms utilizing new electronic equipment controls in the printing sector limit the use of craftworkers to machine set-up. This enables printers to substitute operators with specialized skills for the craftworker trained in the complete process.

Contracts for locals in New York City establish that the work rules of the GCIU require at least one craftworker to set-up and operate all automatically fed press and bindery equipment in union plants.

In 1967, by representing nearly 60 percent of the industry production workers, the ITU and GCIU dominated the craft-oriented commercial printing industry. As the established suppliers of industry skills, the ITU and GCIU sought to maintain control of traditional craft functions by limiting new process operations to craftworkers. The influence of requiring a higher proportion of craftworker employment in union plants is to reduce rather than maintain the membership of the ITU and GCIU. Without recognizing that the craftworker is the exception in traditional journeyman functions, there is no reason to expect that the membership of the ITU and GCIU will not continue to decline.

POSTSCRIPT: TRENDS SINCE 1983

The purpose of this printing industry case study is to determine the long-term relationship between technology, skill, and union membership between 1958 and 1983. Attempts to completely update this study for the three-year period ending in 1986 are thwarted by both the publication lag and discontinuation of publication of data on training, employment, and union membership. Nevertheless, what incomplete information is available does support the three hypotheses that explain the decline in commercial printing industry union membership.

The long-term decline in craft skill level from 1950 to 1980 has stablized, as measured by the years of training required of printing craft workers. The length of nonunion apprenticeships declined between 1950 and 1970, then remained constant at least until 1980 when the data series was discontinued (Table 3.2). Similarly, the years of training required in union craft apprenticeship remained constant in the period 1971–82 (Table 3.1). Comparable union contracts indicate that there has been no change in the length of typesetting, preparation, and press apprenticeship training between 1980 and 1986.[24]

In addition to skill level stabilization, Bureau of Labor Statistics (BLS) data indicate the total proportion of craftworker employment is also stabilizing. Combined craft employment as a percentage of total commercial printing industry employment has remained constant for composition, preparation, and press operators between 1980 (Table 3.12) and the latest available data in 1982. Looking into the future, occupational employment of typesetters will further decline by 1.3 to 2.8 percent in the 13 years 1982–95. Offsetting the decline in typesetting, employment of preparation and press craftworkers will increase 1 percent to total 26 percent of industry SIC 275 employment during the same 13–year period.[25]

The total labor market, competitive to union printers, is continuing to increase (Table 3.10). Commercial printing industry production employment continued to increase from 319,900 to 360,900 between 1983 and 1985. While no data are published, a recent GATF publication suggests that in-plant employment is still increasing. On the basis of the latest Department of Commerce establishment data, quick printing employment increased from 34,272 to 44,155 between 1983 and 1986.[26]

Relative wage data necessary to quantify the union response to skill reducing technology are no longer available. Nationwide union occupational wage rates, published by the BLS, were discontinued in 1980 (Tables 4.6 and 4.7). New York nonunion employer association occupational wage rates were only published until 1982 (Table 5.11). Support for the inverse relation between relative union wages and membership since 1983 would require new indices of relative union/non-union occupational wage rates.

Union membership continued to decline between 1983 and 1985. Combined ITU and GCIU commercial branch membership declined 9 percent between 1983 and 1985. ITU paid membership declined 12 percent from 14,200 to 12,540 in the two years since 1983 (Table 5.5). GCIU commercial membership declined 8 percent from 85,000 to 77,832 between 1983 and 1985 (Table 5.10).[27]

NOTES

1. Bureau of Labor Statistics, U.S. Department of Labor, *Employment and Earnings in the United States: 1907–1978*, and *Supplement to Employment and Earnings*, July 1984, (Washington, DC: U.S. Government Printing Office).

2. U.S. Department of Labor. Bureau of Labor Statistics. *Directory of National Unions and Employee Associations*, 1979, bulletin 2079 (Washington, DC: GPO, 1980), 105 (hereafter cited as *Directory of Unions and Associations*).

3. Bruno, 8/24; Llamas, 7/22; and Robert L. Schweiger. Personal correspondence with the author, 31 August 1983. (hereafter cited as Schweiger, 8/31).

4. James E. Horne. Telephone interview with the author, 1 March 1984.

5. Printing Industries of America, Inc., "Selected Trends of the ITU," Industrial Relations Special Studies Series, (Arlington, VA: Printing Industries of America, 1980), 2. (hereafter cited as "Selected Trends").

6. Seybold, *Modern Photocomposition*, 72; and GATF, *Forecast*, 10, 26, 114.

7. Seybold, *Modern Photocomposition*, 33–5; and Barnett, *Chapters*, 3.

8. Baker, *Printing*, 7, 209, 211.

9. Nelson Eldred. Telephone interview with the author, 6 September 1983. (hereafter cited as Eldred, 9/6); Romano, 9/16; and Seybold, 9/16.

10. GATF. *Forecast* 9, 14.

11. "Merger," *Union Tabloid: The Newspaper of the Graphic Arts Union*, June 30, 1983, 1.

12. Horne, 8/24.

13. Charles R. Cook and Theodore C. Collins, "Letterpress and Lithographic Printing Presses in Place in the United States," *Printing and Publishing,* (July 1962):11, (hereafter cited as "Presses in Place").

14. James E. Horne. Interview with the author, 1 March 1984; and William Solomon. Telephone interview with the author, 18 May 1985. Solomon is president, Graphic Arts Employers of America, Printing Industries of America, Inc.

15. "Contract for Book and Job Work Between Printers' League Section, Printing Industries of Metropolitan New York, Inc. and New York Printing Pressmen's Union, No. 51," for the period 1957–59, "Journeyman Wage Scales," 3–24, Part IX: "Character of Work," 44, and Part X: "Complement of Men," 41; "Contract for Book and Job Work Between Printers' League Section, Printing Industries of Metropolitan New York, Inc. and New York Printing Pressmen's Union, No. 51," for period 1981–83, "Journeyman Wage Scales," 2–10, and Part XIV: "Complement of Men," 64–8; "Contract for Book and Job Work Between Printers' League Section, Printing Industries of Metropolitan New York, Inc. and New York Papercutters and Bookbinders Union No. 119B–43B," for period 1956–58, "Wage Scales, A–H, Part X: "Complement of Men," 18; and "Contract for Book and Job Work Between Printers' League Section, Printing Industries of Metropolitan New York, Inc. and New York Papercutters and Bookbinders Union, No. 119B–43B," for the period 1984–86, "Wage Scales," 4–7, Part X: "Complement of Equipment," 44–5.

16. James E. Horne. Interview with the author, 24 August 1983. Dennis Molloy. Telephone interview with the author, 7 July 1985. Jack Simich, Telephone interview with author 14 October 1985.

17. National Association of Printers and Lithographers. *Sheetfed Economics: 1972–82,* Teaneck, N.J.: NAPL, 1983, 5 Michael Coulson, Telephone Interview, 11 October, 1985. "Contract for Book and Job Work between Printers' League Section, Printing Industries of Metropolitan New York, Inc., and New York Printing Pressmen's Union, No. 51. Effective 8, 1972", 6. "Contract for Book and Job Work between Printers' League Section, Printing Industries of Metropolitan New York, Inc. and New York Printing Pressmen's Union, No. 51 for the period 1981–1983." 19–20, 66.

18. Jack Simich. Telephone interview with the author, 21 March 1983. James E. Horne. Interview with the author, 24 August 1983.

19. Mulvey, *Trade Unions,* 63.

20. National Association of Printers and Lithographers. *NAPL Digitization* (Teaneck, NJ: National Association of Printers and Lithographers, 1983), 4, 44 (hereafter cited as *Digitization).*

21. L. W. Wallis, Electronic Typesetting (Gateshead, UK: Paradigm Press, 1984), 104–5.

22. GATF. *Future of Color,* 110–16; and NAPL. *Digitization,* 20–2.

23. R. M. Schaffert, "Electrophotography Yesterday, Today and Tomorrow," *Photographic Science and Engineering,* 22 (No.3): 151–52.

24. "Scale of Prices, Book and Job Work" as amended January 1, 1983 between New York Typographical Union No. 6 and Printers' League Section, Printing Industries of Metropolitan New York, Inc., p. 81; "Shop Rules and Wage Scales Contract for Book and Job Work," between Printers' League Section, Printing Industries of Metropolitan New York, Inc. and New York Typographical Union, No. 6, commencing October 4, 1975, 77–78; "Shop Rules and Wage Scales Contract for Book and Job Shops" between Printers' League Section Printing Industries of Metropolitan New York, Inc. and Printing and Graphic Communications Union, Local No. 51, 1981–83 and 1983–86.

25. U.S. Department of Labor, *Bureau of Labor Statistics Handbook of Methods, Volume 1,* Bulletin 2134–1 (December 1982) 25–26; U.S. Department of Labor, BLS, unpublished and subject to revision data "Employment by Industry and Occupation 1982 and Projected 1995 Alternatives—Commercial Printing" 1983, page 788.

26. United States Department of Labor, BLS, *Supplement to Employment and Earnings* (Washington: GPO, 1986); Graphic Arts Technical Foundation Market Research Newsletter, Number 10, June 1986 "A Profile of the In-Plant Printer"; U.S. Department of Commerce, Bureau of Industrial Economics, *Franchising in the Economy 1981–1983* (Washington: GPO, 1983) p. 52; U.S. Department of Commerce, International Trade Administration, *Franchising in the Economy, 1984–1986.* (Washington: GPO, 1986) p. 58.

27. Printing Industries of America, Graphic Arts Employers of America Division, "Industrial Relations Bits and Pieces," January 3, 1986, p. 3. Commercial branch is 33 percent of total ITU membership. GCIU commercial branch membership is estimated by weighing both the relative size of the IPGCU and GAIU at the time of their 1981 merger with the component unions' percent of commercial membership. Expert opinion estimated that 36 percent of Printing and Graphic Communications Union (IPGCU) and 80 percent of Graphic Arts International Union (GAIU) were employed in SIC 275, commercial printing.

APPENDIX:

Data Sources and Notes to Tables

The following additional source information and notes are presented for those readers wishing to do further investigation on data presented in the tables throughout the book. Tables not appearing here are complete in text.

Table 2.1
Electrophotography
Xerox Corp., "The Story of Xerography" (Rochester, NY: Xerox Corp., 1978).
Xerox Corp., *1983 Fact Book* Rochester, NY: Xerox Corp., 1983).

Offset Duplication
William Friday, *Quick Printing Encyclopedia* (So. Lake Tahoe, CA: Prudential, 1982).
Donald Daniels provided information on this subject in a personal interview.

Digital CRT (Cathod Ray Tube) Typesetter
John W. Seybold, *Fundamentals of Modern Photocomposition* (Media, PA: Seybold, 1979).
Frank J. Romano provided information on this subject in a personal interview.

Table 2.2
Porte Publishing Co., *Franklin Offset Catalog* (Salt Lake City, UT: Porte, 1983).

Table 2.3
Porte Publishing Co., *Franklin Offset Catalog*. This is the source of conventional offset unit cost data.
William Friday provided photo-direct unit cost data in a personal interview.

Table 2.4

Porte Publishing Co., *Franklin Offset Catalog.* Conventional unit cost data are taken from this catalog.

Howard K. Britt, "The Upheaval in Copy/Duplication," *The New England Printer and Publisher* (July 1978): 20–36. This article contains the Canadian government unit cost data for both conventional offset and electrostatic printing.

William Friday provided data on electrostatic unit costs in a personal interview.

Table 3.1

Collective bargaining agreements for the years indicated in the table between the Printers' League Section of the Printing Industries of Metropolitan New York and Typographical Union Local No. 6, Pressmen's Local No. 51, and Bindery Union Local No. 119B–43B GAIU.

Table 3.2

Printing Industries of Metropolitan New York, Inc., Master Printers' Section, "Recommended Standards of Wages and Hours," published annually, 1958–82.

Table 3.3

U.S. Department of Labor, Bureau of Labor Statistics (USDL, BLS), "Occupational Employment in the Commercial Printing Industry" (Washington, DC: GPO, March 1970),and USDL, BLS, "Employment and Relative Standard Error of Selected Occupations (Commerical Printing Industry, SIC 275)," in *Occupational Employment Survey of Manufacturing Industries* (Washington, DC: GPO, 1977, 1980).

Table 3.4

Printing Industries of Metropolitan New York, Inc., Master Printers' Section, "Recommended Standards of Wages and Hours," published annually, 1958–82.

USDL, BLS, "Occupational Employment in the Commercial Printing Industry"; and USDL, BLS "Employment and Relative Standard Error of Selected Occupations."

Table 3.5

Porte Publishing Co., "Section D. Copy, Negative, Plates and Press Work," *Franklin Offset Catalog, 1965–84.*

Table 3.9

International Resource Development, *In-Plant Printing in the Age of Corporate Electronic Publishing* (Norwalk: International Resource Development, 1984), pp. 21, 42–43.

Table 3.10

Commercial Printing Employment, SIC 275

USDL, BLS, *Employment and Earnings in the United States, 1909–1978,* bulletin 1312–11 (Washington, DC: GPO, 1979). See also supplement to this publication, revised establishment data, published in July 1984.

Private Printing Employment

International Resource Development, *In-Plant Printing in the Age of Corporate Electronic Publishing,* pp. 21, 42–43.

Quick Printing Employment

U.S. Department of Commerce, Bureau of Industrial Economics (U.S. DC, BIE), *Franchising in the Economy 1981–1983* (Washington, DC: GPO, 1983), pp. 21–31.

Table 3.11

These data were compiled on September 9, 1983 by George Silvestri of the BLS on the basis of the 1950, 1960, and 1970 census of population and the *Occupational Employment Statistics Survey of Manufacturing Industries,* 1980. The projection of data to 1990 were made on the basis of data developed by experts at the Department of Labor. The percentages for each craft are comparable to total industry employment data published in *Employment and Earnings in the United States: 1909–1978.*

Table 3.12

USDL, BLS, "Estimated Employment, Standard Error and Percentage of Establishments Reporting Selected Occupations from a Sample Survey of the Commercial Printing Industry (SIC 275)," *Occupational Employment Statistics Survey* (Washington, DC: GPO, 1970, 1980).

Table 3.13

Commercial Printing Employment

USDL, BLS, "Estimated Employment, Relative Standard Error and Percentage of Establishment Reporting Selected Occupations from a Sample Survey of the Commercial Printing Industry (SIC 275)"; and USDL, BLS, "Employment and Relative Standard Error of Selected Occupations, Commercial Printing Industry (SIC 275)."

USDL, BLS, *Employment and Earnings in the United States, 1909–1978,* bulletin 1312 and supplements (Washington, DC: GPO, 1979, 1981, 1983).

Private Printing Employment
International Resource Development, *In-Plant Printing in the Age of Corporate Electronic Publishing,* pp. 21, 42–43.

Quick Printing Employment
USDC, BIE, *Franchising in the Economy 1981–1983,* pp. 21–31.

Table 3.14
Printing and Publishing Employment
USDL, BLS, "Occupational Employment in the Commercial Printing Industry"; and USDL, BLS, "Employment and Relative Standard Error of Selected Occupations (Commercial Printing Industry, SIC 275)."
USDL, BLS, *Employment and Earnings in the United States, 1909–1978,* bulletin 1312 and supplements.

Private Printing Employment
International Resource Development, *In-Plant Printing in the Age of Corporate Electronic Publishing,* pp. 21, 42–43.

Quick Printing Employment
USDC, BIE, *Franchising in the Economy 1981–1983,* pp. 21–31.

Manufacturing Employment
U.S. Department of Commerce, Bureau of Census (USDC, BC), "Occupation by Industry," *1970 Census of Population* (Washington, DC: GPO, 1972), PC(2) 7C; and USDC, BC, *1980 Census of Population,* PC (8-2-7C).

Table 3.15
Electrophotography
Xerox Corp., "The Story of Xerography," pp. 7–8.
Xerox Corp., *1983 Fact Book,* pp. 8–9.

Offset Duplication
William Friday, *Quick Printing Encyclopedia,* p. 360.
Donald Daniels provided information in a personal interview.

Digital CRT Typesetter

John W. Seybold, *Fundamentals of Modern Photocomposition* (Media, PA: Seybold Publications, 1979), p. 139.

Frank J. Romano and John Seybold provided information in personal interviews.

Craft Skill Index Value

Printing Industries of Metropolitan New York, Master Printers' Section, "Recommended Standards of Wages and Hours."

USDL, BLS, "Occupational Employment in the Commercial Printing Industry."

USDL, BLS, "Employment and Relative Standard Error of Selected Occupations (SIC 2275)." Since three digit occupational employment data are not available prior to 1970, this table assumes that industry occupational ratios remained constant between 1966 and 1970.

Relative Hourly Earnings

USDL, BLS "Production Workers Average Hourly Earnings—in Dollars," *Employment and Earnings* (Washington, DC: GPO, July 1984), pp. 22, 215.

Table 3.16

Printing Industries of Metropolitan New York, Inc. Master Printers Section, "Recommended Standards of Wages and Hours."

USDL, BLS, "New York City Manufacturing Average Hourly Earnings," *Employment and Earnings, States and Areas, 1939–1983*, Vol. 2 (Washington, DC: GPO, 1984), p. 579.

Table 4.2

Union Photocomposition Wage Rate

"Contract for Book and Job Work between New York Typographical Union No. 6 and Printers' League Section, New York Employing Printers Association, Inc., 1959–1961," p. 47.

Contract for Book and Job Work between New York Typographical Union No. 6 and Printers' League Section, Printing Industries of Metropolitan New York, Inc., 1975–1982 supplement, "New Journeymen Wage Rates, Effective Shifts Worked or Paid for beginning April 1, 1979," p. 1.

Union Pressman Wage

"Contract for Book and Job Offices between Printers' League Section, New York Employing Printers Association, Inc., and New York Printing Pressmen's Union No. 51, 1959–1962," p. 10.

Contract for Book and Job Shops between Printers' League Section Printing Industries of Metropolitan New York, Inc. and Printing and Graphic Communications Union, Local No. 5, 1981–1983," p. 17.

"Nonunion Wages for Bindery Hand/Machine and General Unskilled".

Master Printers' Section, New York Employing Printers Association, Inc., "Recommended Standards of Minimum Wages and Hours." Approved by the membership at a special meeting, December 10, 1959," p. 2.

Master Printers' Section, Printing Industries of Metropolitan New York, Inc., "Recommeded Standards: Part I Wage Section," 1982 supplement. Approved by the Board of Directors, November 10, 1981, p. 2.

Table 4.3
Commercial Printing Employment
USDL, BLS, "Occupational Employment in the Commercial Printing Industry, March 1970," and "Employment and Relative Standard Error of Selected Occupations, Commercial Printing (SIC 275)."

Union Membership
Courtney D. Gifford, *Directory of U.S. Labor Organizations,* 1984–1985 edition (Washington, DC: Bureau of National Affairs, Inc., 1984), pp. 51–55.

Table 4.4
Commercial Printing Employment
USDL, BLS, "Estimated Employment, Relative Standard Error and Percentage of Establishments Reporting Selected Occupations"; and USDL, BLS, "Employment and Relative Error of Selected Occupations: Commercial Printing Industry (SIC 275)."

In-Plant Printing Employment
International Resource Development, Inc., *In-Plant Printing in the Age of Corporate Electronic Publishing,* pp. 21, 42–43.

Quick Printing Employment
USDC, BIE, *Franchising in the Economy 1981–1983,* pp. 21–31.

Union Membership
Courtney D. Gifford, *Directory of U.S. Labor Organizations,* pp. 51–55.

Table 4.5
Commercial Printing Employment
USDL, BLS, *Employment and Earnings in the United States, 1907–1978,* bulletin 1312 and supplements.

Union Membership
Courtney D. Gifford, *Directory of U.S. Labor Organizations,* pp. 51–55.

Tables 4.6 and 4.7
USDL, BLS, *Union Wages and Hours: Printing Industry,* July 1, 1958
(bulletin 1247); July 1, 1963 (bulletin 1399); July 1, 1967 (bulletin
1592); July 1, 1972 (bulletin 180); September 1, 1978 (bulletin
2049); and September 2, 1980 (bulletin 2125). Publication of union
wage data was discontinued with the 1980 issue.
USDL, BLS, "Production Workers Average Hourly Earnings—in Dollars," *Employment and Earnings,* bulletin 1312–11.

Table 4.8
USDC, BC, "Selected Statistics for Operating Manufacturing Establish-
ments by Type of Operation and Legal Form of Organization for
Major Industry Groups and Industries" (Washington, DC: GPO,
1980), pp. 2–7.
USDC, BC, *Type of Organization, 1977 Census of Manufacturers,*
MC77–SR–7; and *1982 Census of Manufacturers,* MC82–55
(Washington, DC: GPO, 1980, 1985).

Table 4.9
USDL, BLS, *Directory of Labor Unions in the United States,* bulletin
937 (Washington, DC: GPO, 1948), pp. 20, 37, 40, 49.
USDL, BLS, *Directory of National and International Labor Unions in
the United States,* bulletin 1222 (Washington, DC: GPO, 1957),
pp. 31, 39, 40, 45.
USDL, BLS, *Directory of National Unions and Employee Associations*
(Washington, DC: GPO, 1979), pp. 30, 41.

Table 4.10
USDL, BLS, "Average Union Hourly Wage Rates in Printing Trades by
City and Population Group, July 1, 1985," table 8 in *Union Wages
and Hours: Printing Industry,* bulletin No. 1247 (Washington, DC:
GPO, 1959).
USDL, BLS, "Average Wage Rates: Branch and Population Group,"
table 11, *Union Wages and Benefits: Printing Trades,* bulletin
2125 (Washington, DC: GPO, 1982). The last issue of this publication appeared in 1982.

Table 4.13
USDC, BC, "Table 4. General Statistics for Metropolitan and Statistical
Areas, Counties and Selected Cities, 1967 and 1963," *1967 Census
of Manufacturing Area Statistics* (Washington, DC: GPO, 1971).

USDC, BLS, "Table 6, Statistics by Selected Industry Group and Industry for Standard Metropolitan Statistical Areas: 1977 and 1972," and "Table 7, Statistics for Selected Industry Group and Industry for Selected Counties: 1977 and 1972," *1977 Census of Manufacturers,* (Washington, DC: GPO, 1981).

USDC, BC, "Table 6. Statistics by Selected Industry Group and Industry for Metropolitan Statistical Areas: 1982"; and "Table 7, Statistics by Selected Industry Group and Industry for Selected Counties: 1982," *1982 Census of Manufacturers.*

Table 5.2

Courtney D. Gifford, ed., *AFL-CIO Membership Data: Directory of United States Labor Organizations,* 1984–85 edition (Washington, DC: Bureau of National Affairs, Inc., 1982), pp. 51–55.

USDL, BLS, *Employment and Earnings in the United States, 1907–1978,* bulletin 1312 and supplements.

Table 5.3

USDL, BLS, "Estimated Employment, Relative Standard Error and Percentage of Establishments Reporting Selected Occupations," 1970, 1980 editions, *Occupational Employment Statistics Survey: Manufacturing Industries.*

Note: Composing room occupations were classified into craft or other semiskilled occupations on the basis of functions that the union reserves for the exclusive jurisdiction of full journeymen. For example, only a journeyman is permitted to set up a machine. A nonjourneyman may operate a machine. According to a letter from Brian McDonald, Chief of the Division of Occupational Statistics, the revised SIC manual for 1972 reclassified lithographic platemaking services from SIC 275 to SIC 279. This change was reflected in *The Occupational Employment Statistics Survey,* 1977. This survey is the Bureau of Labor Statistics' primary system for collecting occupational data. The year 1971 is the earliest such data are available for all manufacturing industries except for the printing and publishing industries, which were surveyed separately in 1970.

Table 5.5

Digital CRT Typesetter Introduction

This information was obtained from Frank J. Romano and John W. Seybold in personal interviews.

Typesetting Skill Index
"Recommended Standards of Wages and Hours" as approved by the
Master Printers' Section of the Printing Industries of Metropolitan
New York. This annual publication is the source of the number of
years of craft apprenticeship required between 1947 and 1982.
USDL, BLS, "Occupational Employment in the Commercial Printing
Industry."
USDL, BLS, "Employment and Relative Standard Error of Selected
Occupations (Commercial Printing Industry, SIC 275)." Since
three-digit occupational employment data are not available prior to
1970, this table assumes that industry occupational ratios remained
constant between 1966 and 1970.

Typesetting Employment
USDL, BLS, "Estimated Employment, Relative Standard Error and
Percentage of Establishment Reporting Selected Occupations,"
1970, 1980.

Union Membership Data
Courtney D. Gifford, ed., *AFL-CIO Membership Data.*

Table 5.6
USDC, Business and Defense Services Administration, *Economic Summary: Printing and Allied Industries,* vol. 2, no. 8 (Washington, DC: GPO, 1961).

Note: Table 5.6 is developed on the basis of a survey conducted by the
U.S. Department of Commerce. The survey consisted of plants with
50 or more employees in ten selected industry classifications, plus a
small number of other establishments the output of which was so
specialized that a record of their equipment was necessary.
  This survey was conducted under authority granted in Section
705 of the Defense Production Act of 1950, as amended. This act
provides for the collection of information needed in national emergencies. The detailed plant data obtained and tabulated for maximum usefulness under emergency conditions is available to the government for industrial mobilization purposes. Contemplated uses
for this data include a search for facilities able to produce an essential printed product even when demand for it had outstripped normal supply, and locating facilities to which vital production could
be transferred after the original production area had been knocked
out by an enemy attack.
  The survey was conducted by questionnaire. The reporting
form listed standard equipment in various categories by size and,

where appropriate, by process. Provisions were made to report equipment not included on the printed form. Respondents were also asked to supply information on the number of employees, product specialization, and annual gross receipts. Questionnaires were mailed and results were tabulated by the Bureau of the Census as the collecting agency for the Business and Defense Services Administration.

Budget limitations confined the survey to plants employing 50 or more persons. Selection of industry classification was dictated by two considerations: the amount of equipment likely to be found in the industry, and the information already available on the industry's equipment. Newspapers, for example, were included because of the existence of adequate compilations.

Table 5.8

USDL, BLS "Estimated Employment, Relative Standard Error, and Percentage of Establishments Reporting Selected Occupations," 1970; and "Employment and Relative Error of Selected Occupations: Commercial Printing Industry (SIC 275)," 1980.

Table 5.9

USDC, BC, "Letterpress and Lithographic Printing Presses in Place in the United States by the State and Region," by Charles R. Cook and Theodore C. Collins, in *Printing and Publishing Industry Report* (Washington, DC: GPO, 1964).

Note: Data were compiled from two industry surveys conducted in 1958 and 1960. The survey for 1985 was confined to establishments employing 50 or more persons, except for a few small plants having specialized equipment capable of producing essential printed products. The 1,634 establishments covered by the survey produced approximately 60 percent of the output of all plants. The survey for 1960 covered 1,497 establishments and was generally confined to plants employing between 20 and 49 workers. These plants accounted for 25 percent of the output of the total plants surveyed. The industries surveyed were: printing (2732); commercial printing except lithographic (2751); commercial printing, lithographic (2752); engraving and plate printing (2753); manifold business forms manufacturing (2761); greeting card manufacturing (2771); book binding (2789); typesetting (2791); photo-engraving (2793); and electric typing and stereotyping (2794). Data from the two surveys were added to form the various categories for the table.

Table 5.10
Electrophotography Introduction
Xerox Corp., "The Story of Xerography."
Xerox Corp., *1983 Fact Book.*

Photo-Direct Offset Introduction
William Friday, *Quick Printing Encyclopedia,* p. 360.
Donald Daniels also provided data in a personal interview.

Preparation, Press, and Bindery Craft Employment Data
USDL, BLS, "Estimated Employment, Relative Standard Error and
    Percentage of Establishments Reporting Selected Occupations,"
    1970; and "Employment and Relative Error of Selected Occupa-
    tions: Commercial Printing (SIC 275)," 1980.

Printers' Craft Skill Index
"Recommended Standards of Wages and Hours," as approved by the
    Master Printers' Section of the Printing Industries of Metropolitan
    New York.
USDL, BLS, "Occupational Employment in the Commercial Printing
    Industry"; and "Employment and Relative Standard Error of
    Selected Occupations (Commercial Printing Industry, SIC 275).

Union Membership Data
Courtney D. Gifford, ed., *AFL-CIO Membership Data.*

Table 5.11
Printing Industries of Metropolitan New York, Inc., Master Printers
    Section, "Recommended Standards of Wages and Hours," pub-
    lished annually, 1958–82.
"Contract for Book and Job Work Between New York Typographical
    Union No. 6 and Printers' League Section, New York Employing
    Printers Association," between 1958 and 1982.
"Contracts for Book and Job Offices Between Printers' League Section,
    New York Employing Printers Association and New York Printing
    Pressmen's Union No. 51," between 1958 and 1982.

Note: The union compositors' rates are published in the various editions
    of "Contract for Book and Job Work Between Printers' League Sec-
    tion, Printing Industries of Metropolitan New York, Inc. and the
    New York Typographical Union No. 6." Journeyman compositors
    innclude the hand and machine classification since 1958. The
    hourly rate is the weighted average of Monday through Thursday
    and Friday day scale. Local No. 6 contract includes a cost of living

adjustment during the life of the contract. Cost of living increases during the previous contract are included in the rates set by the contracts for 1959, 1961, 1963, 1970, 1974, and 1975.

The union strippers' and pressmen's wage scales are published in the annual editions of "Contract for Book and Job Offices between Printers' League Section, New York Employing Printers Association, Inc. and the New York Pressmen's Union Local No. 51." For purposes of comparison with nonunion scales, the hourly day scales on single- and two-color offset presses were used. The hourly rate is the weighted average of Monday through Thursday and Friday day scales.

BIBLIOGRAPHY

BOOKS AND REPORTS

Allen, R. C. D., *Macro-Economic Theory,* New York: St. Martin's Press, 1968.

Andrews, E. W., *Employment Trends in the Printing Trades,* Chicago: Science Research Associates, 1939.

Atherton, Wallace N., *Theory of Union Bargaining Goals,* Princeton, NJ: Princeton University Press, 1973.

Baker, Elizabeth Faulkner, *Printers and Technology: A History of the International Printing Pressmen and Assistants Union,* New York: Columbia University Press, 1957.

————*Displacement of Men by Machines,* 1933. Reprint, edited by Leon Stein, Salem, NY: Ayer Co., 1977.

Barnett, Charles, *Chapters on Machinery and Labor,* Cambridge, MA: Harvard University Press, 1926.

Battelle Columbus Division. *Interaction of Markets and Technology on Graphic Communications: 1980–1985 Expectations and Opportunities,* Arlington, VA: Printing Industries of America, Inc., 1980.

Beaumont, Richard A., and Ray B. Helgath, *Management, Automation, and People,* New York: Industrial Relations Counselors, 1964.

Bloom, Gordon F., and Herbert R. Northrup, *Economics of Labor Relations,* Homeward, IL: Richard D. Irwin, 1981.

Cartter, Allan W., *Theory of Wages and Employment.* 1944. Reprint, New York: Augustus M. Kelly, 1966.

Chandler, Margaret K., "Craft Bargaining Power," in *Frontiers of Collective Bargaining,* edited by John Dunlop and Neil W. Chamberlain, Chicago: University of Chicago Press, 1977.

Clifford, Courtney D., ed., *AFL-CIO Membership Data: Directory of United States Labor Organizations,* 1982-1983 ed., Washington: Bureau of National Affairs, Inc., 1982.

Craypo, Charles, "The Decline of Union Bargaining Power," in *New Directions in Labor Economics and Industrial Relations,* Washington, DC: Bureau of National Affairs, Inc., 1982.

Drake, Leonard A., *Trends in the New York Printing Industry,* Philadelphia, PA: University of Pennsylvania Press, 1949.

Dunlop, John T., *Wage Determination Under Trade Unions.* 1944. Reprint. New York: Augustus M. Kelly, 1966.

Durbin, Harold C., Terminology, *Printing and Computers,* Easton, PA: Durbin Associates, 1974.

Eagly, Robert V., *The Structure of Classical Theory,* New York: Oxford University Press, 1974.

Eastman-Kodak Company. *Kodak Graphics Industry Manpower Study,* Rochester, NY: Eastman-Kodak Company, 1973.

Edwards, Richard, *Contested Terrain,* New York: Basic Books, Inc., 1979.

Friday, William, *Quick Printing Encyclopedia,* South Lake Tahoe, CA: Prudential Publishing Company, 1982.

Gordon, David M., Richard Edwards, and Michael Reich, *Segmented Work, Divided Workers,* New York, New York: Cambridge University Press, 1982.

Graphic Arts Technical Foundation. *Techno-Economic Forecast 8, The Future of Color Printing: 1979–1980,* Pittsburgh, PA: Graphic Arts Technical Foundation, 1978.

——*Techno-Economic Forecast 9, Prepress Automation: Opportunities 1980–1984,* Pittsburgh, PA: Graphic Arts Technical Foundation, 1979.

——*Techno-Economic Forecast 10: Impact of New Technology on Graphic Arts Work Forces: 1980–1984,* Pittsburgh, PA., Graphic Arts Technical Foundation, 1980.

——"Niche No. 1 Report," Graphic Arts Technical Foundation, Pittsburgh, PA. Photocopy.

——*Annual Report,* Pittsburgh, PA: Graphic Arts Technical Foundation, 1983.

Gustafson, W. Eric., "Printing and Publishing," in *Made in New York: Case Studies in Metropolitan Management,* Max Hall, ed., Cambridge, MA: Harvard University Press, 1959.

Hall, Max, ed., *Made in New York: Case Studies in Metropolitan Management,* Cambridge, MA: Harvard University Press, 1959.

International Paper Company, *Pocket Pal,* New York, NY: International Paper Company, 1979.

International Resource Development, Inc., *In-Plant Printing,* Norwalk, CT. International Resource Development, Inc., 1984.

Hicks, J. R., *The Theory of Wages,* London: Macmillan and Company, Limited, 1935.

Jackson, Robert May, *The Formation of Craft Labor Markets,* Orlando, FL,: Academic Press, Inc., 1984.

Kelber, Harry and Carl Schlessinger, *Union Printers and Controlled Automation,* New York: The Free Press, 1967.

Klasnic, Jack, *Inplant Printing Handbook,* Salem, NH: GAMA Communications, 1981.

Lester, Richard A., *The Economics of Labor,* 2d ed., New York: Macmillan Publishing Co., Inc., 1964.

Lewis & Co., A. F. *Blue Book Marketing Information,* New York: A. F. Lewis & Co., 1981.

Lipset, Seymour, Martin Trow, and James Coleman, *Union Democracy,* New York: The Free Press, 1956.

Loft, Jacob, *The Printing Trades,* New York: Farrar & Rinehart, Inc., 1944.

Mansfield, Edwin, *The Economics of Technological Change,* New York: W. W. Norton & Company, 1968.

———*Microeconomics,* New York: W. W. Norton & Company, Inc., 1970.

Marshall, Alfred, *Principles of Economics,* vol. 1, 9th (Varioum) ed., with annotations by G. W. Guillebaud, London: Macmillan and Company, Limited, 1961.

Muller, Eva, *Technological Advance in an Expanding Economy,* Ann Arbor, MI: University of Michigan Press, 1969.

Mulvey, Charles, *The Economic Analysis of Trade Unions,* New York: St. Martin's Press, 1967.

Munson, Fred C., *Labor Relations in the Lithographic Industry,* Cambridge, MA: Harvard University Press, 1968.

National Association of Printers and Lithographers. *Word Processing's Impact on Today's Typesetting,* Teaneck, NJ: National Association of Printers and Lithographers, 1982.

————"How Developments in Reproduction Technology Are Affecting Markets," NAPL special report, Teaneck, NJ: National Association of Printers and Lithographers, 1983.

————*New Developments in Reproduction Technology Are Affecting Markets,* Teaneck, NJ: National Association of Printers and Lithographers, 1983.

————*NAPL Digitization,* Teaneck, NJ: National Association of Printers and Lithographers, 1983.

————*Sheet Fed Economics: 1972–1982,* Teaneck, NJ: National Association of Printers and Lithographers, 1983.

National Composition Association. Division of the Printing Industries of America, Inc. "Bench Mark Production Reports," Arlington, VA: National Composition Association, 1983.

New York State Department of Labor. *Labor Market Information Handbook for Occupational Planners and Administrators in New York State,* Albany, NY: New York State Department of Labor, 1980.

Porte Publishing Company. "Instructions and Information," section C. In *Franklin Offset Catalog,* Salt Lake City, UT: Porte Publishing Company, 1980.

————"Hour Rates, Negatives, Flats, Plates, Presswork, Photo Composition, etc.," section D. In *Franklin Offset Catalog,* Salt Lake City, UT: Porte Publishing Company, 1983.

Printing Industries of America, Inc. "Selected Trends of the ITU," Industrial Relations Special Studies Series, Arlington, VA: Printing Industries of America, Inc., 1980.

Rees, Albert, *The Economics of Trade Unions,* Chicago: University of Chicago Press, 1977.

Reynolds, Lloyd G., *Labor Economics and Labor Relations,* 8th ed., Englewood Cliffs, NJ: Prentice-Hall, Inc., 1982.

————*The Structure of Labor Markets,* New York: Harper & Brothers, 1951.

Rodgers, Theresa F., and Natalie S. Friedman, *Printers Face Automation,* Lexington, MA: Lexington Books, 1980.

Romano, Frank J., *Printing Industry Trends Almanac,* Arlington, VA: Printing Industries of America, Inc., 1980.

Seybold, John W., *Fundamentals of Modern Photocomposition,* Media, PA: *Seybold Publications,* 1979.

Slichter, Sumner H., James J. Healy, and E. Robert Livernash, *The Impact of Collective Bargaining on Management,* Washington, DC: The Brookings Institution, 1960.

Smith, Anthony, *Goodby Gutenberg,* New York, NY: Oxford University Press, 1980.

Stieber, Jack, ed., *Employment Problems of Automation and Advanced Technology,* New York: St. Martin's Press, 1966.

Stigler, George J., *The Organization of Industry,* Chicago: University of Chicago Press, 1968.

Strauss, Victor, *The Printing Industry,* Arlington, VA: Printing Industries of America, Inc., 1967.

Ulman, Lloyd, *The Rise of the National Trade Unions,* Cambridge, MA: Harvard University Press, 1962.

Union Employers of America. "The Future—People and Technology," Special Study Series, Arlington, VA: Printing Industries of America, Inc., 1983.

U. S. Department of Commerce. Bureau of the Census. *Census of Population,* Washington, DC: GPO, 1960.

————National Bureau of Standards. *Automatic Typographic Quality Typesetting Techniques: A State of the Art Review,* monograph 99, Washington, DC: GPO, 1967.

————Bureau of the Census. *Census of Population,* Washington, DC: GPO, 1970.

————Office of Federal Statistical Policies and Standards. *Employment Outlook,* Washington, DC: GPO.

————Bureau of the Census. *Standard Industrial Classification Manual.* Washington, DC: GPO, 1972.

————Bureau of the Census. *1977 Census of Manufacturers,* Washington, DC: GPO, 1980.

————Bureau of the Census. *Type of Organization, 1982 Census of Manufacturers,* Washington, DC: GPO, 1985.

————Bureau of the Census. *Commercial Printing and Manifold Business Forms, 1982 Census of Manufacturers,* Washington, DC: GPO, 1985.

U. S. Department of the Interior, U. S. National Resources Committee, *The Structure of the American Economy,* Washington, DC: G.P.O., 1939.

U. S. Department of Labor. Wages and Hours Division. *Economic Factors Bearing on Minimum Wages in the Printing and Publishing and Allied Graphic Arts Industry,* Washington, DC: GPO, 1942.

————Bureau of Apprenticeship and Training. *National Apprenticeship and Training Standards for the Graphic Arts International Union.* Washington, DC: Bureau of Apprenticeship and Training, 1981.

————Bureau of Labor Statistics. *Employment Outlook in Printing Occupations,* bulletin 1126, Washington, DC: GPO, 1951.

————Bureau of Labor Statistics. *Occupational Employment in the Commercial Printing Industry,* Washington, DC: GPO, 1970.

————Bureau of Labor Statistics. *Union Wages and Hours: Printing Industry, July 1, 1958,* bulletin 1247, table 5: "Average Union Hourly Wage Rates in the Printing Trades, July 1, 1958, and Increases in Rates July 1, 1957—July 1, 1958" (Washington, DC: GPO, 1959).

————Bureau of Labor Statistics. *Union Wages and Hours: Printing Industry, July 1, 1963,* bulletin 1399, table 6: "Average Wage Rates and Increases by Trade" (Washington, DC: GPO, May 1964).

————Bureau of Labor Statistics, *Union Wages and Hours: Printing Industry, July 1, 1967,* bulletin 1592, Washington, DC: GPO, 1968.

————Bureau of Labor Statistics. *Union Wages and Hours: Printing Industry, July 1, 1972,* bulletin 180, Washington, DC: GPO, 1972.

————Bureau of Labor Statistics, *Union Wages and Benefits: Printing Trades, September 1, 1978,* bulletin 2049, Washington, DC: GPO, 1980.

————Bureau of Labor Statistics, *Union Wages and Hours: Printing Industry, September 2, 1980,* bulletin 2125, Washington, DC: GPO, September 1982.

————Bureau of Labor Statistics, *Employment and Earnings in the United States: 1909-1978*, Washington, DC: GPO, 1979.

————Bureau of Labor Statistics, *Supplement to Employment and Earnings*, Washington, DC: G.P.O., 1984.

————Bureau of Labor Statistics, "Survey of Manufacturing Industries." In *Occupational Employment Statistics*, Washington, DC: GPO, 1980.

————Bureau of Labor Statistics, *Directory of National Unions and Employee Associations*, Washington, DC: GPO, 1980.

————Bureau of Labor Statistics, *Occupational Employment in the Commercial Printing Industry*, Washington, DC: GPO, 1980.

————Bureau of Labor Statistics, *Metropolitan Areas, United States and Regional Summaries*, bulletin 1950-77, Washington, DC: GPO, 1980.

————Bureau of Labor Statistics, "Printing and Publishing," by Robert V. Critchlow, in *The Impact of Technology on Labor in Five Industries*, bulletin 2137, Washington, DC: GPO, 1982.

Wallis, L. W., *Electronic Typesetting*, Gateshead, UK: Paradigm Press, 1984.

Weber, Arnold R., "Collective Bargaining and the Challenge of Technological Change," in *Industrial Relations: Challenges and Responses*, edited by John G. Crispo, Toronto: University of Toronto Press, 1966.

Xerox Corporation, *1983 Fact Book*, Stamford, CT: Xerox Corporation, 1983.

Zimbalist, Andrew, ed., *Case Studies on the Labor Process*, New York: Monthly Review Press, 1979.

JOURNAL AND TRADE PERIODICAL ARTICLES

Brett, Howard K., "The Upheaval in Copying/Duplicating," *The New England Printer and Publishing* (July 1978): 28, 32, 54.

Brown, Kenneth J., and Alexander J. Rohan, "Union Labor 1973," *Inland Printer/American Lithographer*, 170(5): 42.

Bureau, William H., "Copying/Duplicating Methods Through the Years," *Graphic Arts Monthly*, (December 1977): 77–79.

Cook, Charles R., "Major Centers of Commercial Printing," *Printing and Publishing* (Fall 1981): 15.

Cook, Charles R., and Theodore C. Collins, "Letterpress and Lithographic Printing Presses in Place in the United States," *Printing and Publishing* (July 1962): 11.

Correia, Joseph G., "Mergers in the Printing and Publishing Industries," *Printing and Publishing* (Fall 1968): 130.

Dertouzos, James N., and John H. Pencavel, "Wage and Employment Determination Under Trade Unionism: The International Typographical Union," *Journal of Political Economy*, 8 (December 1981): 1179–1180.

Dunlop, John T., and Benjamin Higgins, "Bargaining Power and Market Structure," *Journal of Political Economy*, L(1): 2–3.

Gennard, John, and Steve Dunn, "The Impact of New Technology on the Structure and Organization of Craft Unions in the Printing Industry," *British Journal of Industrial Relations*, XXI(1).

Giebel, Gregory, "Corporate Structures, Technology and the Printing Industry," *Labor Studies Journal* (Winter 1979): 235.

Griffin, Tony, "Technological Change and Craft Control in the Newspaper Industry: An International Comparison," *Cambridge Journal of Economics*, 8 (March 1984): 44–46.

Lofquist, William S., "Shipments Concentration in the United States Printing and Publishing Industry," *Printing and Publishing* (Winter 1981/1982): 3, 7.

————"Mergers and Acquisitions in the United States Printing and Publishing Industry," *Printing and Publishing* (Summer 1978): 3, 7.

Scharfert, R. M., "Electrophotography Yesterday, Today and Tomorrow," *Photographic Science and Engineering*, 22(3): 151.

Schweiger, Robert L., "Today's Quick Printers Are Tomorrow's Commercial Printers," *Quick Printing* 7(4): 36.

Semling, Jr., Harold V., "Trade Unions Eye Merger Route As Path to National Unity," *Printing Management* (February 1974): 33.

Stern, James L., "Automation—and/or a New Day in Unionism," *Annals of the American Academy of Political and Social Science*, vol. 350 *The Crisis of American Trade Unions* (November 1969): 25–35.

U.S. Department of Commerce. "Transportation Patterns of Printed and Published Products." Prepared by Dorothy Hokkanen. *Printing and Publishing* (October 1970): 10.

————Business and Defense Services Administration. "Letterpress and Lithographic Printing Presses in Place in the United States by State and Region," Quarterly Industry Report prepared by Charles R. Cook and Theodore C. Collins, *Printing and Publishing* (July 1964): 7–10.

Wallis, Robert, "Automation and Restrictive Labor Agreements," *Printing World* 188(18): 394.

INTERVIEWS AND PERSONAL COMMUNICATIONS

Anderson, Richard. Interviews with the author, New York, 7 April 1983, and 24 August 1983.

Baker, Robert. Telephone conversation with the author, 1 July 1983.

Bruno, Michael. Telephone conversation with the author, 24 August 1983.

Cook, Brian S. Letter to the author, 30 March 1984, and telephone conversation with the author, 6 April 1984.

Cook, Charles R. Telephone conversation with the author, 20 July 1983.

Coulson, Michael. Letter to the author, 24 May 1984, and telephone conversation with the author, 11 October 1985.

Daniels, Donald. Telephone conversation with the author, 30 September 1983.

DeMinco, Marcia A. Letter to the author, 8 December 1983.

Eldred, Nelson. Letter to the author, 8 April 1983, and telephone conversation with the author, 6 September 1983.

Friday, William. Telephone conversation with the author, 16 January 1984.

Gill, Brian. Telephone conversation with the author, 13 July 1983.

Horne, James E. Interviews with the author, 7 April 1983, 11 April 1983, 28 June 1983, 24 August 1983, 1 March 1984; letter to the author, 16 April, 1984.

Llamas, J. Telephone conversation with the author, 1 July 1983.

Luca, Raymond J. Letter to the author, 14 March 1984.

Molloy, Dennis. Telephone conversation with the author, 6 May 1983.

Piercy, Donald. Telephone conversation with the author, 13 July 1983.

Ramstad, Donald. Telephone conversation with the author, 25 July 1983.

Ray, Ford. Telephone conversation with the author, 15 September 1983.

Romano, Frank. Telephone conversation with the author, 15 September 1983.

Scheldrick, Joseph. Telephone conversation with the author, 15 September 1983.

Schweiger, Robert L. Letter to the author, 31 August 1983.

Seybold, John W. Telephone conversation with the author, 16 September 1983.

Silvestri, George. Telephone conversation with the author, 28 December 1983.

Simich, Jack. Telephone conversations with the author, 21 March 1983, 13 April 1983, 28 June 1983, 30 June 1983, 8 August 1983, 25 August 1983, 15 September 1984.

Snow, Elman. Letter to the author, 9 January 1984.

Trieste, John. Interview with the author, 24 August 1983.

UNION CONTRACTS

"Contract for Book and Job Work Between Printers' League Section, Printing Industries of Metropolitan New York, Inc. and New York Typographical Union No. 6" for period 1955–57.

"Contract for Book and Job Work Between Printers' League Section, Printing Industries of Metropolitan New York, Inc. and New York Papercutters and Bookbinders Union No. 119B–43B" for period 1956–58.

"Contract for Book and Job Work Between Printers' League Section, Printing Industries of Metropolitan New York, Inc. and New York Printing Pressmen's Union, No. 51" for period 1957–59.

"Contract for Book and Job Work Between Printers' League Section, Printing Industries of Metropolitan New York, Inc. and New York Typographical Union No. 6" for period 1967–70.

"Contract for Book and Job Work Between Printers' League Section, Printing Industries of Metropolitan New York, Inc. and New York Typographical Union No. 6" for period 1974–75.

"Contract for Book and Job Work Between Printers' League Section, Printing Industries of Metropolitan New York, Inc. and New York Typographical Union No. 6" for 1975.

"Contract for Book and Job Offices Between Printers' League Section, Printing Industries of Metropolitan New York, Inc. and Graphic Arts International Union No. 119B-43B" for period 1976–78.

'Contract for Book and Job Offices Between Printers' League Section, Printing Industries of Metropolitan New York, Inc. and Printing and Graphic Communications Union No. 51, IP & GCU–AFL–CIO" for period 1977–78.

"Contract for Book and Job Work Between Printers' League Section, Printing Industries of Metropolitan New York, Inc. and New York Printing Pressmen's Union No. 51" for period 1981–83.

"Contract for Book and Job Work Between Printers' League Section, Printing Industries of Metropolitan New York, Inc. and New York Typographical Union No. 6" for period 1983–89.

"Contract for Book and Job Work Between Printers' League Section, Printing Industries of Metropolitan New York, Inc. and New York Papercutters and Bookbinders Union, No. 119B–43B" for period 1984–86.

NEWSPAPER ARTICLES

"President's Talk Details ITU Goal," *International Typographical Union Review*, 24 (No. 16): 1.

"Bingel: Be Proud of Union," *International Typographical Union Review*, Conv. Is., (1981): 1.

"North America's Largest Graphic Arts Union Created in Vote Avalanche by 81% of GAUI and 78% of IPGCU," *Union Tabloid* (30 June 1983): 1.

"Merger," *Union Tabloid* (30 June 1983): 1.

"No Matter What You Publish or Print—Copiers Are Gaining on You," *Vectors* (January 1984): 1.

MEMORANDA

Printing Industries of Metropolitan New York, Inc., Master Printers' Section "Recommended Standards of Wages and Hours" published annually, 1958–82.

Sommer, Donald E., "The Role of Open Shops in the Printing Industry," (26 January 1973): 3.

Index

A. B. Dick Company, 28, 34, 44, 63, 134
acquisition, 108
AFL/CIO, 19, 87
ALA, 13, 19, 111, 112, 123
Amalgamated Lithographers of America (ALA), 13, 19, 112; disaffiliation of with AFL/CIO, 111, 123; membership, 112, 113
American Federation of Labor/Congress of Industrial Organizations (AFL/CIO), 19, 87
American Type Founders, 28
Anderson, Richard, 53, 81
apprenticeship, 50, 51–52; demise of, 106; nonunion assistant pressman, 51; specialization, 146
apprenticeship requirements, 53; nonunion, 54; union, 53
apprenticeship training, 26, 52
automation, 27; advances in, 24
automatic plate developing, 42, 43
automatic press feeding, 26, 132
automatic process control, introduction of, 2

Baker, Elizabeth, 132
Baker, Robert, 64
bargaining power, 14
binary electronic data processing, 12
binderies, 51, 164; as adjuncts of pressroom, 134
bindery machine setter, 77
bindery workers, 25, 66; classification of, 97; decline in wages,

57, 82; industry agreements, 96; unskilled, 77
blanket cylinder, 44
bookbinders, 25; relative earnings, 82; specific occupational titles, 77
bottle machine: automatic, 11; semiautomatic, 11, 15
Britt, Howard K., 155
Brown, Kenneth J., 88, 91, 93

camera/platemaker, 34–35, 43
camera skills, 2, 27
Carlson, Chester, 36
cathode ray tube (CRT) photocomposition, 8, 24, 26, 28, 29–33, 79, 107, 154, 157; advantages, 31–32; competition, 70; definition, 29; history and source, 29–31
Census, Bureau of, 77, 90
Census of Manufacturers, 112, 131
Chapters on Machinery and Labor (Barnett), 8, 11, 12, 15, 18
cold type new machinery shipments, ratio of hot type to, 131
collective bargaining, 55
collective bargaining agreements, 106, 155; plant relocation and, 111; union hourly wage data defined, 101–2; union training requirements in, 52
color printing, 143; craft employment increase and, 59–62; skill-intensive, 78

177

About the Author

Daniel T. Scott is president of Scott Printing Corporation, a full-service printing establishment with over 200 employees. He has more than 20 years' professional experience in the printing industry, and has drawn on this first-hand knowledge of the printing unions for the present study.

Dr. Scott holds a Ph.D. in Economics from the New School for Social Research (1986), an MBA in Corporate Finance from New York University (1969), and a BA in Economics from Notre Dame University (1966).

He is active in the Graphic Communications Association, serving as its director from 1982 to 1985, and is director of the Hudson County Chamber of Commerce.